"Eight expert theologians here elucidate and constructively build upon the sacramental-liturgical essays of Marie-Dominique Chenu, one of the most important but lesser-known figures in the *ressourcement* movement that shaped the documents of Vatican II and the ensuing renewal of the church and sacraments. I expect that, like myself, readers of this volume will arrive at a deep sense of gratitude—gratitude for Chenu's courageous, learned, pastoral, and generative work. But gratitude, also, for this colloquium's critical advancement of Chenu's fecund insights into the bodily, symbolic, ritual character of liturgy, joining nature and mystery, anthropology and theology, history and revelation, culture and tradition."

—Bruce T. Morrill, SJ, distinguished professor of theology,
Vanderbilt University Divinity School

"This book offers a refreshing, perspective-rich, new look at a largely unknown Chenu."

—Christian Bauer, University of Münster

"What a gift this book promises to be for the discipline of liturgical studies. Chenu was one of the trailblazing thinkers behind the liturgical renewal of Vatican II. He interpreted Aquinas with fresh eyes, confidently speaking from his (Chenu's) own historical context. The editors and contributors take their cue from Chenu's own priority of time, history, and the body in the study of sacraments and sacramentality. Publishing the five essays in English under one cover and including the thoughtful critique of eight contemporary scholars embodies Chenu's own methodology of doing theology while keenly aware of the signs of the times. This book will be read and reread for years to come."

—Judith M. Kubicki, CSSF, associate professor emerita,
Fordham University

The Worshiping Body

Chenu, Liturgy and Sacraments

Edited by
Joris Geldhof, Samuel Goyvaerts, and Tom McLean

LITURGICAL PRESS
ACADEMIC

Collegeville, Minnesota
litpress.org

Cover photo: Marie-Dominique Chenu in Rome during the Second Vatican Council. Courtesy of the Archives of the Dominicans of the Province France/ Tangi Cavalin, Nathalie Viet-Depaule (dir.), online biographical dictionary of the Dominican Fathers.

Cover design by David Drummond.

Library of Congress Cataloging-in-Publication Data

Names: Chenu, Marie-Dominique, 1895-1990. Works. English. Selections. | Geldhof, Joris, 1976- editor. | Goyvaerts, Samuel, 1986- editor. | McLean, Thomas (Thomas Paul), editor.
Title: The worshiping body : Chenu, liturgy and sacraments / edited by Joris Geldhof, Samuel Goyvaerts, and Tom McLean.
Description: Collegeville, Minnesota : Liturgical Press Academic, [2025] | Includes bibliographical references. | Summary: "French Dominican Marie-Dominique Chenu (1895-1990) was an important visionary of Catholic theology in the 20th century. The basis of this book is formed around five texts on liturgy and sacraments by Chenu, now available in English translation for the first time. The translations of these articles are alongside essays by expert scholars on contextualized themes that surface in Chenu's essays"-- Provided by publisher.
Identifiers: LCCN 2025000583 (print) | LCCN 2025000584 (ebook) | ISBN 9798400802058 (trade paperback) | ISBN 9798400802065 (epub) | ISBN 9798400802072 (pdf)
Subjects: LCSH: Chenu, Marie-Dominique, 1895-1990. | Catholic Church--Liturgy. | Sacraments--Catholic Church. | Theology--France.
Classification: LCC BX4705.C46358 W67 2025 (print) | LCC BX4705.C46358 (ebook) | DDC 264.02--dc23/eng/20250305
LC record available at https://lccn.loc.gov/2025000583
LC ebook record available at https://lccn.loc.gov/2025000584

Contents

Original Publications

"Anthropology and Liturgy" was originally published as: Marie-Dominique Chenu, "Anthropologie et liturgie," *La Maison-Dieu* 12 (1947): 53–65.

"The Sacraments in the Christian Economy" was originally published as: Marie-Dominique Chenu, "Les sacrement dans l'économie chrétienne," *La Maison-Dieu* 30 (1952): 7–18.

"Faith and Sacrament" was originally published as: Marie-Dominique Chenu, "Foi et sacrement," *La Maison-Dieu* 71 (1962): 69–77.

"Anthropology of the Liturgy" was originally published as: Marie-Dominique Chenu, "Anthropologie de la liturgie," in *La liturgie après Vatican II: Bilans, études, prospective*, ed. Jean-Pierre Jossua and Yves Congar (Paris: Cerf, 1967), 159–77.

"For a Sacramental Anthropology" was originally published as: Marie-Dominique Chenu, "Pour une anthropologie sacramentelle," *La Maison-Dieu* 119 (1974): 85–100.

Introduction

Tom McLean

Marie-Dominique Chenu (1895–1990) has perhaps become something of a forgotten figure, at least compared to the leading lights in the changes and developments in Catholic theology in the lead-up to, during, and in the immediate aftermath of the Second Vatican Council. Nonetheless, he should stand as one of the founding figures of the renewal of Catholic theology in the twentieth century. His "lasting achievement" was to dethrone a singular standard reading of Thomas Aquinas's *Summa Theologiae* as the only accepted way of doing Catholic theology, leading to the expansion of the field toward its current form.[1] While he is particularly renowned for his work on Aquinas, framed by his historical study of the twelfth and thirteenth centuries, Chenu ranged across the breadth of theology—ironically in a way in which his (and his contemporaries') revolution in the field has now made impossible. He engaged substantially with the themes of contemplation and incarnation,[2] as well as addressing the contemporary questions about work and the church's social teaching.[3] The

1. Fergus Kerr, *Twentieth-Century Catholic Theologians: From Neoscholasticism to Nuptial Mysticism* (Malden, MA: Blackwell, 2007), 32.

2. Cf. Christophe Potworowski, *Contemplation and Incarnation: The Theology of Marie-Dominique Chenu*, McGill-Queen's Studies in the History of Ideas 33 (Montreal: McGill-Queen's University Press, 2001).

3. Marie-Dominique Chenu, *The Theology of Work: An Exploration*, trans. Lilian Soiron (Chicago: Henry Regnery, 1966); Marie-Dominique Chenu, *La "doctrine sociale" de l'Église comme idéologie* (Paris: Cerf, 1979).

importance he gave to engaging with "the signs of the times,"[4] both in study of historical approaches to theology and in the life of the church and study of theology today, was eventually given prominent place by the council at the heart of *Gaudium et Spes*.

Nonetheless, the works of Yves Congar, Henri de Lubac, Hans Urs von Balthasar, Karl Rahner, Joseph Ratzinger, and Edward Schillebeeckx are all much better known and more widely studied. Chenu, in contrast, is often more remembered as a locus of controversy—noted for his removal from his teaching position at the Dominican study house Le Saulchoir, and then for his exclusion from an official role as a *peritus* at Vatican II—than for the distinctive contributions he made.

In keeping with this inattention, the origins of this project in fact do not lie in the study of the work of Chenu, but instead that of Schillebeeckx. In the 1990s, when researching and planning a new book on sacramental theology—one which he never got to finish before his own death in 2009—Schillebeeckx returned to an article by his old theological mentor published in 1974.[5] Upon finding an annotated copy of this article in the archive of Schillebeeckx's papers from this work in the Katholiek Documentatie Centrum at Radboud University in Nijmegen, it was clear to us that Chenu's own thought was as worthy of further study as Schillebeeckx's developing new insights.

This 1974 essay picked up by Schillebeeckx was not Chenu's only writing on the topic of sacramental theology; instead, it was the last of five essays written over a period of nearly four decades. Four of them were originally published in what was then and remains the leading liturgical journal in French Catholic theology, *La Maison-Dieu*, at first published by the *Centre de pastorale liturgique*, and then later by the *Service national de pastorale liturgique et sacramentelle*. The other was first published in a volume of essays edited by Congar and Jean-Pierre

4. See Mary Kate Holman, *Marie-Dominique Chenu: Catholic Theology for a Changing World* (South Bend, IN: Notre Dame Press, 2025).

5. Schillebeeckx's one published essay from this work, however, does not mention Chenu; see Edward Schillebeeckx, "Naar een herontdekking van de christelijke sacramenten: Ritualisering van religieuze momenten in het alledaagse leven," *Tijdschrift voor Theologie* 40 (2000): 164–87; ET: Edward Schillebeeckx, "Towards a Rediscovery of the Christian Sacraments," in *Essays: Ongoing Theological Quests*, The Collected Works of Edward Schillebeeckx 11 (London: Bloomsbury, 2014), 183–210.

Jossua in immediate response to the call for liturgical reform made by the council in the first document it promulgated, *Sacrosanctum Concilium*.[6] In this volume, we offer the five of them together for the first time in English translation, along with a series of essays responding to them from different perspectives.

This introduction strives to serve two functions: first, to introduce why there is merit in theological reflection retrieving the thought of Chenu today; and second, to draw together some of the insights that will emerge in the essays that follow.

Why Read Chenu Today?

I want to begin with one of the central pillars Chenu draws from Thomas Aquinas: that God provides for created beings according to the particular form of their being.[7] This, Chenu reminds us, is the first part of St. Thomas's argument for the necessity of the sacraments, but also underpins the entire understanding of divine gift and grace in the Angelic Doctor's thought. On the basis of this fundamental principle, both time and history, and the body become essential for Chenu.

Time and History

As Holman observes in her essay in this volume, Chenu's concern for time and history runs against the highly speculative, highly metaphysical, background of the work of Chenu's doctoral mentor Réginald Garrigou-Lagrange. Both in his doctoral study on contemplation and in his books on Thomas Aquinas, Chenu considered it "essential for reaching St. Thomas's thought to put it back in the milieu where it was born"[8] His critique of his *Doktorvater* and others of the same mindset

6. Jean-Pierre Jossua and Yves Congar, eds., *La liturgie après Vatican II: Bilans, études, prospective* (Paris: Cerf, 1967).

7. Chenu 1974, par. 2. Cf. *ST* IIIa, q. 61, a. 1, resp.: "In a manner corresponding to its own particular way of functioning." ET: Thomas Aquinas, *The Sacraments: 3a. 60-5*, ed. David Bourke, vol. 56, *Summa Theologiae* (Cambridge: Cambridge University Press, 2006).

8. Carmelo Giuseppe Conticello, "'De Contemplatione' (Angelicum, 1920): La thèse inédite de doctorat de P. M.-D. Chenu," *Revue des sciences philosophiques et théologiques* 75 no. 3 (1991): 363–422, at 386; ET from Holman in this volume. A more complete

for their reading of Thomas's work as "a perennial philosophy" can also be repeated here.[9] Thomas, and Thomas's thought, for Chenu, must be considered in the context, in the history, in which he lived and it was developed. But this is only part of how Chenu calls us to a more historically rooted theology. Yes, the sources should be read in historical context, but also the acts of the doing of theology and of the life of Christians and of the church cannot be removed from the moment of history, the moment of time in which they stand.

And so, in the same mindset, we cannot pretend—however desirable it might sometimes seem—that the liturgical action takes place outside time. Of course, we cannot pretend that because the form of the liturgy is the product of historical development we can fully understand it by studying that history alone, for all the venerable work done by historians of the liturgy. And certainly it might (or even: should, and possibly: must) imply and contain what some ritual theorists, borrowing from linguistics, call the subjunctive mood, a "what if" quality, which imagines what the (eschatological) future will look like. But above all, each celebration occurs in that specific moment in time which we call the present. It is not apart from time: it is too *human* an activity for that. It is not the heavenly liturgy of the angels, set apart from the temporal progression of our world, but activity in time. It is not a fixed product of some golden age, be that in the early church, or the fourth century, or the Carolingian or Tridentine reforms.[10] We can turn, as Speelman indicates in his contribution here, to the

---

version of the thesis has been published as Marie-Dominique Chenu, "'De Contemplatione": Thèse de doctorat, Angelicum, 1920," *Revue des sciences philosophiques et théologiques* 105, no. 4 (2021): 537–676, https://doi.org/10.3917/rspt.1054.0537; for Chenu's work on Aquinas, see Marie-Dominique Chenu, *Toward Understanding Saint Thomas*, trans. Albert M. Landry and Dominic Hughes (Chicago: Henry Regnery, 1964); and Marie-Dominique Chenu, *Aquinas and His Role in Theology*, trans. Paul Philibert (Collegeville, MN: Liturgical Press, 2002); as well as the brief article Marie-Dominique Chenu, "The Plan of St. Thomas' *Summa Theologiae*," trans. Ellen Bremner, *Cross-Currents* 2, no. 2 (1952): 67–79.

9. Marie-Dominique Chenu, *A School of Theology: Le Saulchoir*, trans. and ed. Joseph A. Komonchak and Mary Kate Holman (Adelaide: ATF Press, 2023), 80.

10. Cf. Paul F. Bradshaw, "Liturgical Reform and the Unity of Christian Churches," *Studia Liturgica* 44, nos. 1–2 (September 2014): 163–71, https://doi.org/10.1177/00393207140441-219.

cosmic liturgy which the temporal, earthly, contingent celebration foreshadows and in which it participates, but not the timeless eternity of angelic worship.[11]

And it is in time because, in accord with temporality of human nature, time and history is where God is revealed, where God is encountered. As such for Chenu, "true religion" and its worship "inserts the personal history of the believer in a holy history . . . but it leaves the human person in their worldly condition, even when sanctifying it."[12] And, for Chenu, central to that understanding of the human condition is the body:

> It is the human condition not to possess a mind except in a body, not to express unchangeable truth except in time, which is where it successively incarnates itself. Revelation has dressed itself in human colors according to the ages in which it was manifested to us.[13]

The Body

A great theme across much of Chenu's work, which we have seen also in these five essays, is incarnation. Perhaps Chenu at times ventures too far and his use of "incarnation" has too little reference to the historical figure of Jesus of Nazareth, certainly compared to the christological works of later figures, such as his student Schillebeeckx.[14] While reintroducing the historical Jesus to theology was undertaken by others, perhaps Chenu merely reintroduced the historical Thomas.[15]

Nevertheless, in the earliest of the essays translated in this volume, it is the human underpinnings of the incarnation that Chenu offers

11. Cf. Chenu 1967, par. 4; Chenu 1974, par. 33.

12. Chenu 1967, par. 15.

13. Chenu, *A School of Theology*, 44; originally published as Marie-Dominique Chenu, *Une école de théologie: le Saulchoir* (Tournai: Kain, 1937); reprinted with commentary, Marie-Dominique Chenu, *Une école de théologie: le Saulchoir*, ed. Giuseppe Alberigo (Paris: Cerf, 1985).

14. Cf. Potworowski, *Contemplation and Incarnation*, 197; and Edward Schillebeeckx, *Jesus, an Experiment in Christology*, The Collected Works of Edward Schillebeeckx 6 (London: Bloomsbury, 2014).

15. Though as Goris points out in this volume, there are a number of ways where this historical Thomas might be as incomplete as a number of presentations of the historical Jesus have been critiqued for being.

as the basis for the sacramental economy.[16] In developing this, Chenu turns both to the corporate, Mystical Body of Christ—and so the social nature of humanity—and to individual human persons. These he keeps fundamentally connected: the embodied human individual shares in the "essentially social nature of humanity." As such, the liturgy—as human celebration—too must be communal, albeit relating to both "the personal and collective life of human beings."[17]

When Chenu focuses on the individual, it is perhaps with greater attention to an abstracted quality of the human person as union of body and soul, rather than to specific embodied human persons. Certainly, it remains a long way from the depth of concern for individual bodies in their very specific gendered forms to which feminist theologies have drawn attention.[18] (And I could add here reference to the other forms of diversity in the human body that are brought to the fore by the likes of decolonial, postcolonial, black, womanist, queer, and other theologies.) Chenu, I suggest, does not intentionally reduce the body to a default of "privileged white cishet male," but is equally not addressing those important questions at all. Nonetheless, a focus on a common core of the embodied human person—shared by those of all races, gender identities, and sexualities—might offer a more productive point of departure than is sometimes articulated in official church discourse that emphasizes a certain set of differences and binaries to narrow ideological ends. Chenu's focus on the human bodies as "the living flesh of the sacraments,"[19] when taken with the space he allows by not seeking to enshrine doctrinally any particular anthropological approach, might offer a start toward this.

In his contribution here, Goyvaerts observes how so often in today's celebrations of the liturgy and in the training of its ministers (at least in the North Atlantic world), attention to the body is so often lacking—we barely even move the bodies of worshipers around the liturgical space, never mind considering the full extent of what part bodies, in all their shapes and sizes, can and do contribute to the full,

16. Chenu 1947, par. 1.

17. Chenu 1947, par. 1.

18. See the contribution of Roll to this volume.

19. Chenu 1967, par. 18.

conscious, and active participation of the worshiper.[20] Or in Chenu's words, we don't consider how "Worship includes in its very substance the reality, burdensome and exciting, of the life of the body, with *all its components*."[21]

This has both corporate and individual implications for the celebration of the liturgy, but as Praud points out in his contribution, we cannot reduce "active participation" to "group facilitation." The faithful response of the many and the faithful, embodied response of the individual are interwoven in the sharing of the tradition of faith.

In some ways, Chenu is more interested in what the body *does* than what it *is*. But this is not a "doing" just as "mechanical execution": the "gesture" at the center of Chenu's concern is an integrated part of the signification process. These gestures can have significant impact on how the mystery is thematized—and not just at the level of academic discourse, but in the continuity of those thematizations down to the "ordinary" believer—as Chenu puts it:

> A certain way of receiving the Eucharistic bread, and already of making it as a "host," dissolves the realism of the meal where one eats, at the same time as it reflects a bad theology of transubstantiation.[22]

The footnote Chenu attaches to this sentence is equally damning of the gesture of baptism using only a drop of water. In both cases the fullness of the gesture, and of the body's interaction with it, is important to its significatory value, whether that conveys a significance that Chenu supports or not.

While it might be reasonably assumed which side of some of our contemporary debates he would sit on, Chenu's framing of these gestures perhaps offers a change of dynamic to the way that such debates are sometimes framed in today's "liturgy wars." There is not a *prima facie* claim that any specific posture or gesture is better—even though Chenu ends up with such a judgment—but instead it is to be placed in the context of the participation of the body as a whole. The

20. Cf. *Sacrosanctum Concilium* 14.
21. Chenu 1967, par. 18; emphasis added.
22. Chenu 1967, par. 20.

gesture to receive communion, the gesture of baptism: both are more than just the special sacramental acts, but also part of a whole matrix of "functional articulations" of the body caught up with "symbolic implications."[23]

There is in the use of this by Chenu a distinction made between a sign, pointing to something else, and a symbol, including the thing signified. In this volume, Goris challenges whether this is faithful to Aquinas's understanding of the category of sign, but for Chenu the distinction seems valuable to respond to the distortions he sees in the dualist tendencies he attributes to the combination of Cartesian and Augustinian thought. The distinction he makes, even if we dispute the terms he uses to do so, is certainly important. No "mere" sign is enough; sacramentality demands a greater depth than that.

Whatever conclusion one actually draws from the Pew Research Center's 2019 survey results about whether Catholics believe the eucharistic elements "actually become" the body and blood of Christ, or are "symbols" thereof,[24] the questions of the meaning of liturgical symbolism and signification remain important and unresolved pastorally. The emphasis on using freshly consecrated eucharistic bread (from a eucharist celebrated that day in the same place or elsewhere) in the recently announced protocols of the Archdiocese of Cologne for communion from the reserved sacrament at Sunday celebrations in the absence of a priest highlights this well because they stand in a stark contrast to the experience of many Catholics around the world who routinely—during the eucharist, and contrary to the intention of the magisterium—receive communion only from the tabernacle.[25] There is a deficient symbolic expression to the liturgical experience today that cannot be ignored when considering, as Pope Francis does

23. Chenu 1967, par. 20.

24. Gregory A. Smith, "Just One-Third of U.S. Catholics Agree with Their Church That Eucharist Is Body, Blood of Christ," *Pew Research Center* (blog), August 5, 2019, https://www.pewresearch.org/short-reads/2019/08/05/transubstantiation-eucharist-u-s-catholics/.

25. Cf. Alexander Saberschinsky, "Liturgiereferent Saberschinsky zur Ermöglichung von Wortgottesfeiern am Sonntag," domradio.de, October 1, 2024, https://www.domradio.de/video/liturgiereferent-saberschinsky-zur-ermoeglichung-von-wortgottesfeiern-am-sonntag.

in his apostolic letter *Desiderio Desideravi*, the contemporary capacity for the liturgy (44–45).

Uniting the Sacred and the Profane

I have already noted Chenu's rejection of a body-soul dualism. While this has a clear anthropological foundation, it is also part of Chenu's profound rejection of the dualism between the sacred and the profane, which itself is intertwined with his emphasis on the incarnation and the action of the sacraments themselves.

This should not be read as a confusion of the sacred with the profane. But the two are, in Chenu's thought, inseparable because there is no human access to the sacred except through the world of matter—the world of the profane. He comes close to Schillebeeckx's controversial maxim here: *extra mundum nulla salus* (outside the world, there is no salvation)—nonetheless, I suspect Chenu would join with Schillebeeckx in placing the emphasis on the *salus*![26]

The recollection from one of Chenu's students in 1968, that they should go out "to make some history,"[27] sits alongside Chenu's emphasis on the importance of contemplation for the theologian.[28] To repeat this in Chenu's own words:

> For a theologian, then, contemplation is not a summit reached now and then by a sudden leap of fervor that takes him out of his study, as if to escape his task and his method. Contemplation is his natural, constitutive milieu, the only place where scientific organization and innovative discovery can occur with singular fruitfulness.[29]

26. Edward Schillebeeckx, *Church: The Human Story of God*, The Collected Works of Edward Schillebeeckx 10 (London: Bloomsbury, 2014), 5ff.; Edward Schillebeeckx, "Letter from Edward Schillebeeckx to the Participants in the Symposium 'Theology for the 21st Century: The Enduring Relevance of Edward Schillebeeckx for Contemporary Theology' (Leuven – 3–6 December 2008)," in *Edward Schillebeeckx and Contemporary Theology*, ed. Lieven Boeve, Frederiek Depoortere, and Stephan Van Erp (London: T&T Clark, 2010), xiv–xv.

27. Matthew Fox, *Confessions: The Making of a Postdenominational Priest*, revised and updated ed. (Berkeley, CA: North Atlantic Books, 2015), 82, as quoted by Holman in this volume.

28. See the contribution of van Erp to this volume.

29. Chenu, *A School of Theology*, 74.

Certainly in his consideration of the nature of theology as a science, this understanding of contemplation is essential to how Chenu holds together rationality and mystery. In another essay, on the nature of theology, Chenu brings together these layers in relation to the sacramental, arguing: "It is the perception of faith—in the case of the sacraments, embodied in ritual prayer and social practice—which is the fundamental source of this rational formulation."[30] Contemplation is not, for Chenu, an open-ended exercise in speculation. It is grounded in the givens of revelation as experienced and lived in the life of the church. *Nulla salus*, neither *extra mundum* nor *extra ecclesiam*!

The task in *Gaudium et Spes* of "examining the signs of the times," and already in Chenu's thought before the promulgation of that document,[31] can be seen as a summary of how to understand the work of discernment that Chenu is pointing to as he brings contemplation and action together.

The relationship which Chenu suggests between theology and the human sciences typifies this bringing together of sacred and profane. Theology is most clearly not a humanities subject for Chenu, whatever the practical arrangements of many universities today might suggest. Nonetheless, his claim that "The more theology is theology, the more the humanities will have a right to intervene in it" remains a remarkable one.[32] There is evidently a fragility to the reciprocal dialogue between disciplines that Chenu is calling for here, but despite the difficulties, if Chenu is correct, then it is essential for good theology. This connection is not because of some methodological principle of the human sciences, and goes beyond the way in which theology should draw upon other scientific disciplines. It is because of their subject: humanity.

In his contribution, van Erp asks about the place of liturgy as a *locus theologicus*. But Chenu's argument here about the relationship between the human sciences and theology has greater potential implications

30. Marie-Dominique Chenu, "What Is Theology?," in *Faith and Theology*, trans. Denis Hickey (Dublin: M.H. Gill and Son, 1968), 26.

31. *Gaudium et Spes* 4. Cf. Holman, *Marie-Dominique Chenu: Catholic Theology for a Changing World*.

32. Chenu 1974, par. 6.

for fundamental theology. This concern for the human, in every sense, has the potential to reframe how we think about the *loci theologici*, of how all of human life can become material for theology, and how processes of humanization are in themselves processes of deification. Chenu almost seems to think—without having explicated a system or a comprehensive fundamental theology—that there is more authority to the human *as human* as a source than is customarily granted. Furthermore, he begins to raise the possibility that the human is more than just a non-proper *locus*, but an inherently theological one.

In this regard, Chenu comes close to positions being raised by post- and decolonial theologies, and may have something to offer in the constructive work that should accompany the necessary critical deconstruction in such approaches. Already familiar with the need to do theology from the margins and with the *damnés*,[33] and having inspired and been inspired by the liberation theology of Gustavo Gutierrez,[34] Chenu might appear an ideal ally in such a pursuit. Although decolonial thought would emphasize the fundamental ambiguity of the human in history and stand opposed to certain normative understandings[35] in ways that would not be immediately familiar to Chenu, his deep attention to the specific realities of the concrete context of Christian believers and practice leaves his work responsive to engage with today's "signs of the times."

Chenu is ultimately a theologian of his own times, shaped by his particular formation and experiences. Yet his reflections on sacraments

33. Cf. Frantz Fanon, *The Wretched of the Earth*, trans. Richard Philcox (New York: Grove Press, 2004).

34. See Holman's paper in this volume.

35. Judith Gruber, "Ambiguïteiten omarmen en onschuld verliezen. Over een paradigmaverschuiving in de theologie," in *De bisschop van Rome en de theologen van Leuven*, ed. Joris Geldhof, Instrumenta Theologica, XLIII (Leuven: Peeters, 2024), 166–67; ET: Judith Gruber, "Papal Visit 2024: Gruber on Pope Francis' Call for a Theological Paradigm Change—Theology Research News," *Theology Research News* (blog), September 30, 2024, https://theo.kuleuven.be/apps/press/theologyresearchnews/2024/09/30/papal-visit-2024-gruber-on-pope-francis-call-for-a-theological-paradigm-change/; on the ambiguity of decoloniality, see Nelson Maldonado-Torres, "Outline of Ten Theses on Coloniality and Decoloniality" (Fondation Frantz Fanon, October 23, 2016), 30, https://www.fondation-frantzfanon.com/wp-content/uploads/2018/10/maldonado-torres_outline_of_ten_theses-10.23.16.pdf.

and sacramentality here offer a perspective that can inform today's reading of the "signs" to help understand what it is in the present day for the embodied faithful to participate in the symbolic gestures of the liturgy, and to encounter "the presence of grace in the mystery."[36] Chenu does not offer ultimate answers but can lead us further into the mystery of humanity in the mystery of sacrament.

The Contributions

When inviting the contributors to this volume, we wanted to draw together a variety of perspectives, with a deliberate desire to include those for whom Chenu and his oeuvre was already well-known, and those who knew him less well. All were invited to read the five essays, and then took part together in a seminar held in Tilburg in Spring 2024. The papers presented here are the fruits of those discussions, and reflect the different perspectives their authors brought to Chenu's texts. We believe these angles offer a pertinent beginning, both as introduction to this aspect of Chenu's work, and to further reflection in sacramental anthropology and theology in light of the "signs of the times."

Mary Kate Holman (Fairfield University) begins our collected work by placing Chenu's five "sacramental" essays in the context of his life and his work. She highlights the key phases of his life in his early formation, his time teaching at Le Saulchoir, his engagement with workers' movements in Paris, and his time at the council and its legacy on him. In this, she emphasizes the importance of his life experience in shaping his theology, and how this is seen too in these essays.

After the translations of Chenu's work, we turn to three essays that explore Chenu's work in relation to some foundational themes. **Olivier Praud** (Institut Catholique de Paris) begins by reflecting on the significance Chenu attaches to the bodily nature of the human person. From Chenu's reaction against spiritualizing tendencies, Praud highlights both the embodied human condition and the irreducible communal consequences of this for liturgical celebration, and their importance for the form of liturgical formation to which Pope Francis points in his apostolic letter *Desiderio Desideravi*.

36. Chenu 1952, par. 26.

Drawing on the connections made by Chenu between liturgical practice, and revelation and sacramentality, **Stephan van Erp** (KU Leuven) argues for the inclusion of the liturgy as a *locus theologicus*. Observing the lack of attention for the liturgical life of the church among fundamental theologians and the growing understanding of liturgical theology by its practitioners as a *theologia prima*, van Erp argues for the revelatory power of the liturgy and its importance as a counter to excessively rationalistic approaches to fundamental theology.

Joris Geldhof (KU Leuven) develops a similarly fundamental question: what it is to move from a theology of the sacraments to doing theology sacramentally. He sees in Chenu important resources to address questions of human capacity for the sacramental in the world today, and thus for the work of theological exposition.

Given Chenu's prominence as a scholar of Thomas Aquinas and the constant reference back to the Angelic Doctor throughout his work, we considered it essential to ask where his thought in these essays stands in relation to the study of Thomas today. **Harm Goris** (Tilburg University), in his contribution here, highlights how Chenu's original way of reading Aquinas, and especially his focus on an *exitus-reditus* schema for the *Summa Theologiae*, shapes his sacramental reflections. Based on more recent reevaluations of Thomas, Goris argues that this causes Chenu to lose sight of some of Aquinas's key reflections on the sacraments as signs and on the sacraments as remedy for sin, neither of which can be forgotten in a search for a coherent theological anthropology.

Chenu's preference to approach sacraments as symbols and mystery, rather than signs, is taken up in a different perspective by **Willem Marie Speelman** (Tilburg University). In conversation with Chenu and Gabriel Marcel, Speelman explores how the "symbolic gesture" of the liturgical celebration expresses and communicates the mystery which it contains and to which it points.

Susan K. Roll (Saint Paul University, Ottawa) reads Chenu's essays through a feminist lens, and while it would be for a large part impossible to call him a feminist, Roll finds significant correlations between the attention to the culture and context in which he writes, and the concerns of feminist theologies over the place of women in the liturgy. Drawing upon Chenu's attention for what is symbolized, Roll invites us also to consider what is simply overlooked.

In the final contribution, **Samuel Goyvaerts** (Tilburg University) finds in Chenu important contributions for contemporary pastoral liturgy. In particular, Chenu's focus on the body provides a framework to move beyond considerations simply of the proper liturgical texts to the wider consideration of the actions that accompany them, the material things used in celebrating them, and the imagination to inhabit them.

The volume concludes with a short afterword from **Karim Schelkens** (Tilburg University), who reflects on how the sacramental draws together many of the threads of Chenu's work that have often been divided.

When referring to the essays of Chenu, the contributors have made use of the paragraph numbers used in this volume. These are not original, but have been added for ease of navigation, either in the translations printed here or for those who wish to refer back to the original French texts. We have made a deliberate choice in our reading of Chenu to translate in a gender neutral fashion with regard to humanity, and, where this does not cause confusion, with regard to God. Thus Chenu's reference to *l'homme* will usually be rendered as *human beings* or *humanity*, rather than by the narrower *man*. More generally, Chenu often makes use of sentence structures that simply do not make sense in English; we have accordingly adapted the structure to preserve as far as we can what seems to be his meaning and emphases in a clear and contemporary English idiom. Nonetheless, for the ease of reference back to his French texts, we have not changed any of the paragraph breaks.

Chenu wrote some of these texts with more extensive footnotes than others, and as he notes in one of them, sometimes they are "reportage" of oral presentations rather than texts prepared for the printed page. We have preserved his footnotes where present, albeit replacing citations of French texts with references to equivalent English editions where these exist. We have also added a number of explanatory footnotes throughout the texts, particularly to aid with the contextualization of them; such additions are introduced with "Translators' note."

Chenu in Context

Mary Kate Holman

Marie-Dominique Chenu was a man of many times. As a historian, his work constantly revisited the past, especially the thirteenth century, his period of expertise. As a theologian, he was deeply immersed in the present, embracing the "signs of the times" as *loci theologici* decades before the Second Vatican Council used that language. For both his historical engagement with the past and his theological engagement with the present, we might now consider him to be ahead of his time, laying groundwork for the future of the church that he himself could not have foreseen.

Chenu was born in 1895 and died in 1990, a lifetime spanning nearly the entirety of the twentieth century.[1] He experienced, responded to, and participated in the massive societal and ecclesial changes of this era, corresponding to five distinguishable periods in his life: his years of formation, his early career at the French Dominican House of Studies (Le Saulchoir), his time living among worker communities in Paris, his contributions to Vatican II, and his twilight years in the postconciliar period. The essays under consideration in this volume fall into the last three periods of his life, but the first two laid the groundwork for those ideas to take shape. This short intellectual biography aims to contextualize themes that surface repeatedly in Chenu's essays on liturgy.

1. Two recent biographies of Chenu expand on the brief insights shared here: Étienne Fouilloux, *Marie-Dominique Chenu 1895–1990* (Paris: Éditions Salvator, 2022), and Michael Quisinsky, *Marie-Dominique Chenu: Weg – Werk – Wirkung* (Freiburg im Breisgau: Verlag Herder, 2021).

The development of Chenu's thought is inextricably tied to his life experience—or to use a word he frequently invokes in his liturgy essays, inextricably tied to his *humanness*. Contextualizing Chenu is an application of his own methodology, as his central scholarly achievement as a historian was to situate Thomas Aquinas in the context of the thirteenth century. Chenu insisted that to understand Thomas, one needed to understand his context. And so, I contend, to understand Chenu, we need to do the same.

Early Life (1895–1920)

Marcel Chenu was born in 1895, just south of Paris in Soisy-sur-Seine, to a working-class family. Few details survive from his childhood. In 1912 he began attending the local diocesan seminary, and he joined the Dominicans a year later at eighteen years of age. With his entry into the order, he took the name Marie-Dominique, which he would use exclusively for the rest of his life.

Chenu's first year of study as a Dominican took place at Le Saulchoir, the French province's house of studies. Due to the *laïcité* laws of 1905, Le Saulchoir had been temporarily relocated to the little Belgian hamlet of Kain, just outside of Tournai. This education in exile allowed for a kind of freedom that transcended the stifling anti-modernism of most seminary education during this period.[2] Although he only spent one year of formation there, Le Saulchoir loomed large in Chenu's imagination and would go on to hold great significance for him.

With the outbreak of the First World War, Le Saulchoir temporarily closed. Exempt from military conscription for health reasons, Chenu spent the remaining five years of his education at the Angelicum in Rome, moving from the exiled margins of small-town Belgium to the epicenter of Roman Catholicism. In 1919, he was ordained a priest. In 1920 he completed a thesis on contemplation in the thought of Thomas Aquinas, mentored by Réginald Garrigou-Lagrange, a Dominican no-

2. See the chapter "Exile Catholicism," in Sarah Shortall, *Soldiers of God in a Secular World: Catholic Theology and Twentieth-Century French Politics* (Cambridge, MA: Harvard University Press), 19–49.

torious for his somewhat rigid metaphysical, speculative Thomism.[3] Chenu's thesis diverged in certain sections from his mentor's approach, representing an early attempt at a historically conscious theological methodology, a commitment that would expand and deepen over the course of his career. He explains in the thesis's section on method, "It is essential for reaching St. Thomas's thought to put it back in the milieu where it was born, where it developed, according to this or that response, under this or that influence."[4] While Garrigou-Lagrange did not appreciate Chenu's moments of historical experimentation in the thesis, there seems to have been a mutual respect between teacher and student during this period. Garrigou-Lagrange invited Chenu to remain at the Angelicum in a teaching position, but Chenu turned this and a second invitation in 1922 down, choosing instead to return as a professor to his beloved Saulchoir.[5]

Le Saulchoir (1920–1942): *Ressourcement* or *nouvelle théologie*?[6]

Upon arrival at Le Saulchoir in 1920, Chenu was named professor of the history of doctrines, and in 1932, he also became Director of Studies. He sought to further develop the educational model set

3. For a more thorough assessment of Chenu's relationship with Garrigou-Lagrange, see Janette Gray, "Marie-Dominique Chenu and Le Saulchoir: A Stream of Catholic Renewal," in *Ressourcement: A Movement for Renewal in Twentieth-Century Catholic Theology*, ed. G. Flynn and P. D. Murray (Oxford: Oxford University Press, 2012), 205–18. For a comprehensive and sympathetic study of Garrigou-Lagrange, see Richard Peddicord, *The Sacred Monster of Thomism: An Introduction to the Life and Works of Reginald Garrigou-Lagrange, OP* (South Bend, IN: St. Augustine's, 2005).

4. Chenu's thesis is only available in excerpt form, in an article published the year after his death. See Carmelo Giuseppe Conticello, "'De Contemplatione' (Angelicum, 1920): La thèse inédite de doctorat du P. M-.D. Chenu," *Revue des sciences philosophiques et théologiques* 75 (1991): 363–422, at 386.

5. André Duval, "Aux origines de 'l'Institut Historique d'Études Thomistes' du Saulchoir (1920 et ss.): Notes et documents," in *Revue des sciences philosophiques et théologiques* 75 (1991): 423–48, at 437–38.

6. The most thorough treatment of this era in Chenu's life is Christian Bauer, *Ortswechsel der Theologie: M. Dominique Chenu im Kontext seiner Programmschrift "Une école de théologie: Le Saulchoir"* (Münster: LIT Verlag, 2011).

in motion by the predecessors he so admired, including Ambroise Gardeil, Antoine Lemmonyer, and Pierre Mandonnet.[7] While most Catholic seminaries at this time were insular clerical communities with pedagogy limited to the memorization of neoscholastic manuals, Le Saulchoir aspired to a more rigorous university style education with a faculty who were not just teachers but also top researchers.

Chenu's own scholarship during this time drew from cutting-edge currents in both theology and secular history. He borrowed strands of the historical-critical method that scholars like Marie-Joseph Lagrange had been developing in biblical studies, applying them to another privileged source of theological wisdom in the Catholic tradition: the texts of Thomas Aquinas. He developed expertise in medieval grammar and rhetoric, writing a series of articles on lexicography and textual and philological analysis of medieval texts—significant contributions to medieval studies, still cited by scholars today. He was also heavily influenced by the *Annales* school, taking great pride in being one of the first subscribers to their journal in 1929.[8] Their attention to economic, political, and cultural conditions would broaden Chenu's research in medieval studies beyond textual work. Yet his approach to history was also deeply theological, always in service of a more profound understanding of the key sources of Christian faith.

Chenu thus emerged as a central figure of the *ressourcement* movement, returning to early Christian sources to revitalize the tradition in its present moment. His abiding commitment to and appreciation of this method appear in the opening paragraphs of both his 1952 and 1962 essays on liturgy. Contemporaries like Henri de Lubac and Jean Danielou sought revitalization in earlier patristic writings, while Chenu turned to Aquinas. Propositional Thomism—a system of ideas

7. For a comprehensive account of Chenu's time at Le Saulchoir, including these influences, see "Introduction" in Chenu, *A School of Theology: Le Saulchoir*, trans. and ed. Joseph A. Komonchak and Mary Kate Holman (Adelaide: ATF Press, 2023), vii–lii.

8. Marie-Dominique Chenu and Jacques Duquesne, *Un théologien en liberté: Jacques Duquesne interrogee le père Chenu* (Paris: Éditions du Centurion, 1975), 51. For a detailed examination of Chenu's reception of the *Annales* method in his early work, see Bauer, *Ortsweschel der Theologie*, 252–93, and Michael Quisinsky, *Geschichtlicher Glaube in einer geschichtlichen Welt: Der Beitrag von M.-D. Chenu, Y. Congar und H.-M. Féret zum II. Vaticanum* (Berlin: Lit Verlag, 2007), 109–12.

abstracted from original texts—reigned in the anti-modernist paradigm of Catholic theology, but Chenu offered a different vision of what it meant to be a disciple of Aquinas. "It is good Thomism," he argued, "to know the history of Thomas' thought, to see his soul united to his body."[9] Xavier Debilly describes Chenu's historical work during this period, as "dusting off medieval texts to restore them in the freshness of their original creation to the twentieth-century reader." This dust consisted of "centuries of reading and commentaries accumulated to the point of becoming a sort of screen between the texts themselves and those who receive them from several centuries of distance."[10] By understanding the way people wrote and thought in the thirteenth century, and the intellectual, economic, political, and religious currents that people were debating in that era, one could better appreciate the theological insight of the Angelic Doctor.

While the past was of central importance to Chenu's vision of theology at this time, so too was the present. After all, if Aquinas engaged the realities of his own time, to be a good Thomist in the twentieth century meant theologians would have to engage the realities of their own era. Chenu felt strongly that good formation for ministry required that future priests understand the world into which they were being sent. Beginning in the early 1930s, he began inviting JOC (Young Christian Workers) for study days at Le Saulchoir, perceiving their mission to the working class as rich material for theological reflection. Around this time, Chenu taught a course for young Dominicans on Marx, which he later acknowledged "may not have been very well done, but it constituted a first awakening."[11] He arranged for students to have nonclerical work experience in nearby communities. In his pedagogy and scholarship, Chenu favored the concrete over the abstract—grounding theological reflection in the quotidian and in the historical. This lifelong commitment shines through clearly in his liturgy essays under consideration in this volume.

9. Chenu, *A School of Theology*, 102.

10. Xavier Debilly, *La théologie au creuset de l'histoire: Marie-Dominique Chenu et son travail avec la Mission de France* (Paris: Cerf, 2018), 68.

11. Chenu and Duquesne, *Un théologien en liberté*, 66.

Chenu articulated the distinctive Saulchoir approach to theological education in a speech for the feast of Thomas Aquinas in 1936, which he went on to publish in 1937 as a short book, *A School of Theology: Le Saulchoir*. With chapters on the history of Dominican education, theology, philosophy, and medieval studies, Chenu argued against the abstraction and dehistoricization of theology found in Thomistic manuals and commentaries. He advocated instead for a historically sensitive return to the foundational texts of Aquinas, "fresh documents whose inexhaustible riches truly earn them the name 'sources.' "[12] *Ressourcement,* indeed.

This little manifesto raised the hackles of fellow Dominicans in Rome, who found his content threatening and his tone dismissive. The anti-modernist paradigm of Vatican-sanctioned theology invoked the eternal relevance of Thomistic truths as a sort of bulwark against the developments of the modern world, so Chenu's embrace of both social realities and an historical approach to Thomas seemed, to some, dangerously relativistic. Chenu agreed in 1938 to travel to Rome to sign his name to ten propositions clarifying positions in his book and confirming his orthodoxy. These tellingly included, "dogmatic formulas state the absolute and immutable truth"; "It is a splendid thing that the Church considers the system of St Thomas to be quite orthodox"; and "One should be respectful in the way one speaks or writes about other approved writers and teachers, even if they are found to fall short in certain respects."[13] Such propositions, scholars have since argued, did not seriously engage the substance of Chenu's arguments, demonstrating what Fergus Kerr calls "fabulous absurdity,"[14] or, for Joseph Komonchak, the "stunning incomprehension of [Chenu's] Roman critics."[15]

While he thought this acquiescent gesture had put the matter to rest, in 1942, with no forewarning, the book was placed on the Index of Forbidden Books; Chenu was removed from his post at Le Saulchoir; and the entire school was subjected to an apostolic visitation. Étienne

12. Chenu, *A School of Theology*, 43.

13. Appendix in Chenu, *A School of Theology*, 107–8.

14. Fergus Kerr, *Twentieth-Century Catholic Theologians: From Neoscholasticism to Nuptial Mysticism* (Malden, MA: Blackwell, 2007), 19.

15. Komonchak, "Introduction," in *A School of Theology*, xxxvi.

Fouilloux argues convincingly that it was Chenu's former mentor, Garrigou-Lagrange, who instigated this melee.[16] In an *Osservatore Romano* article justifying the text's condemnation, Pietro Parente coined the phrase *nouvelle théologie*, intended pejoratively to characterize Chenu's work, as well as that of Louis Charlier. In the climate of anti-modernism, novelty and deviation from the prevailing paradigm was subversive, if not heretical.

Workers in Paris (1942–1954)

Exiled from Le Saulchoir in 1942, Chenu arrived at the Couvent St. Jacques, a Dominican residence in the poor industrial thirteenth *arrondissement* of Paris. He was cut off from his home of the last twenty-two years, removed from the classrooms and libraries where his scholarly career had flourished, and forbidden from teaching theology in ecclesial settings. Yet his theological imagination did not languish. Instead, he found in these Parisian worker communities rich soil for scholarship and ministry, intensifying his interest in social realities that had taken root with the JOC at Le Saulchoir.

Chenu arrived in Paris during a moment of bourgeoning social apostolates. Lay movements like Catholic Action and innovative seminaries like the Mission de Paris and Mission de France sought to evangelize the "dechristianized" French working class who had largely rejected religious practice.[17] Prior to his arrival in Paris, Chenu corresponded with Louis Augros, the founder of the Mission de France, sharing their mutual vision of religious formation that embraced historical consciousness and social commitments. Moving to Paris allowed him to develop more substantial ties to these organizations, especially the more radical Worker-Priest movement.[18]

16. Fouilloux, *Marie-Dominique Chenu 1895–1990*, 116–23.

17. While "dechristianization" is now a contested category, it was the language employed by Chenu and his peers. For a robust history of the Mission de France, see Tangi Cavalin and Nathalie Viet-Depaule, *Une histoire de la Mission de France: La riposte missionnaire 1941–2002* (Paris: Éditions Karthala, 2007).

18. For a thorough history of the movement during this period, see Oscar Arnal, *Priests in Working Class Blue: The History of the Worker-Priests (1943–1954)* (Mahwah, NJ: Paulist Press, 1986).

The Worker-Priests saw the French church's separation of sacred and profane as the key cause of dechristianization, and they envisioned a radical fusion of the two as the means to minister to the working class. They took on full-time manual labor to enter into total solidarity with the people, and found themselves transformed by the experience, re-envisioning what sacramental ministry meant when clerical distinction was almost entirely erased. Although he did not perform full-time manual labor himself, Chenu was in the thick of this movement. The thirteenth *arrondissement*, his own neighborhood, had France's highest geographic concentration of worker clergy. He played a significant advisory role in the movement, leading their retreats and attending their weekly meetings to reflect with them on their experiences, essentially serving as the movement's theologian. He wholeheartedly embraced the movement's insistence that the sacred ought not to be separated from quotidian reality. We see the impact of these experiences in his 1967 "Anthropologie de la Liturgie," animating his argument that the liturgy of an incarnational faith must unite the sacred and the profane.

In addition to more organized movements, Chenu frequented *"les petits foyers,"* gatherings of lay workers in their homes. This pastoral aspect of his career, often overlooked by scholars of his work, deeply impacted his theology. This seems to be the prototype for the kind of "cell communities" Chenu describes in his 1947 essay, "Anthropology and Liturgy." Chenu served as a sort of chaplain and theologian for these families, peeling potatoes if the host couple were running late; listening to and learning from peoples' experiences in their labor unions, political movements, and family support groups.[19] He imbued the quotidian experiences of these people with theological significance, recalling later:

> I would start by listening with both ears to their experiences. . . . These people weren't asking for a solution from on high, they wanted me to help them find Christian solutions for themselves, out of their own experience. And maybe not even solutions in the strict sense of the term, but directions, inspirations, perspectives. In some of these

19. J. and J. Boniface, "Les 'petits foyers' du Père Chenu," in *L'hommage différé au Père Chenu*, ed. Claude Geffré (Paris: Cerf, 1990), 145.

> gatherings, I didn't present myself as a theologian at all, because theology has a reputation of being an esoteric, abstract, unreal, drawn-out science. But after several debates, I would tell them: 'What we just did there—that was theology.' . . . Indeed, we had followed an inductive method out of their own experience.[20]

Chenu embraced this inductive theological method for the rest of his career.[21]

A paradigmatic example is his 1952 article and subsequent 1955 book, *A Theology of Work.* Here we find many resonances with his essays on liturgy, as he meditates on theological anthropology—what it means to be human—in the twentieth-century context of industrial laborers. He critiques an impulse toward irrelevant theologizing that does not understand the reality of the industrial worker, arguing, "Historians can understand the contemptuous reaction of Marx. We must beware of this decaying theology."[22] An undercurrent of incarnation runs through his anthropology, and by extension, his understanding of human work: "God is made man [*sic*]; all that is human is material for grace. If work takes on human consistency, then . . . it becomes part of, enters into the economy of grace."[23] He invites his reader to "see man [*sic*]as collaborator in creation and participant in evolution by his discovering, exploiting and spiritualizing Nature," which entails "divine participation."[24] The reality of twentieth-century labor clarifies this realization, which can really only emerge out of an inductive theological method that takes experience seriously. Chenu's 1967 piece, "Anthropologie de la Liturgie" echoes the insights of *A Theology of Work,* particularly when invoking "the new awareness [humanity] has gained of its existence in history, i.e., of the dimension that its

20. Chenu and Duquesne, *Un théologien en liberté,* 101–2.

21. For a detailed exploration of how Chenu's theology evolved during this period, see Mary Kate Holman, "'Like Yeast in Dough': The Church-World Relationship in the Evolving Thought of Marie-Dominique Chenu," *Theological Studies* 81, no. 4 (2020): 788–809.

22. Chenu, *The Theology of Work: An Exploration,* trans. Lilian Soiron (Dublin: M.H. Gill and Son, 1963), 34.

23. Chenu, *The Theology of Work,* 24.

24. Chenu, *The Theology of Work,* 23.

perfection accomplishes through its active participation in the construction of the world, in the development of society, in the collective advancement of peoples."[25]

While these twelve years in Paris were transformative for Chenu's social consciousness, they would once again subject him to ecclesial scrutiny. In 1949, the Holy Office condemned Christian collaboration with communism of any kind, placing Worker-Priests who belonged to communist labor unions in a precarious position. This political backlash had a theological counterpart in the 1950 encyclical *Humani Generis,* which, although it did not name any specific theologians, rebuked the kind of theological methods Chenu and his peers were undertaking.[26] In 1953, with a variety of tensions brewing between Rome and the Worker-Priest movement, word came that they would no longer be permitted to undertake full-time industrial labor. Chenu drafted an article in defense of the movement, "The Vocation of the Worker-Priest," which certain superiors interpreted as imprudent, impertinent, even perhaps "leading the worker-priests to apostasy."[27]

His entanglement in this drama was part of a larger network of French Dominicans considered highly suspect in Rome. The scholarship published by the Dominican publishing house Cerf, as well as *La Quinzaine,* a weekly leftist magazine affiliated with the Dominicans, came under scrutiny. Vatican officials had also continued to surveil pedagogy at Le Saulchoir in the decade after Chenu's removal. Congar's scholarship on ecumenism, the laity, and ecclesial reform alarmed the Holy Office in the wake of *Humani Generis.* In 1954, Chenu, Congar, Cerf editor Pierre Boisselot, and theologian Henri Férét, were each exiled from their respective assignments. Under immense pressure from Rome, the Spanish Dominican superior Emmanuel Suarez visited France and removed their provincial, violating an 800-year precedent of directly electing Dominican superiors.[28] Chenu specifically was re-

25. Chenu 1967, par. 10.

26. See Joseph A. Komonchak, "*Humani Generis* and *Nouvelle Théologie,*" in *Ressourcement: A Movement for Renewal in Twentieth-Century Catholic Theology,* ed. Gabriel Flynn and Paul D. Murray (Oxford: Oxford University Press, 2012), 138–56.

27. Chenu and Duquesne, *Un théologien en liberté,* 159.

28. See François Leprieur, *Quand Rome condamne: Dominicains et prêtres ouvriers* (Paris: Cerf, 1989), and Thomas O'Meara, "'Raid on the Dominicans': The Repression of 1954," *America* 170, no. 4 (February 5, 1994): 10.

located to Rouen and forbidden from returning more than one week per month to visit the *petits foyers* in Paris. He was removed from the Dominicans' provincial council. His privileges as a master of theology were revoked, and he was explicitly forbidden from teaching at the École des Hautes Études –despite its lack of religious affiliation—as a matter of obedience. His work was put under Roman censure, an experience that compromised his ability to not only write, but also think, freely. The following five years were a rather fallow period for Chenu, what his biographer Étienne Fouilloux calls "the darkest phase of his life . . . the only time when a form of depression seems to have taken away his proverbial optimism."[29]

Vatican II (1959–1965)

Given the two dramatic episodes of censure he had endured, imagine Chenu's surprise when Pope John XXIII announced the Second Vatican Council in 1959, signaling a shift in the church's posture to the modern world. Despite a battered reputation in Rome which precluded him from serving as a *peritus*, Chenu significantly contributed to this monumental event in the life of the Catholic Church. His historically conscious and socially engaged theological method, previously targets of ecclesiastical ire, in fact laid the groundwork for the council's breakthroughs.

Chenu came to Rome as the private theological consultant for Claude Rolland, a former student who had become a missionary bishop in Madagascar. By extension, Chenu became an unofficial expert for the entire African episcopacy. His less formal commitments included assistance to the Melkite Catholics, and membership in the Church of the Poor working group. Chenu's influence at the council was relational and largely informal in nature; his presence at conferences, lunches, and press interviews advanced his ideas when he did not have access to the meetings of official *periti*. His behind-the-scenes involvement is especially clear in two conciliar documents in which he had a hand, and which reflect the central themes of his theology.

29. Étienne Fouilloux, "CHENU, Marie-Dominique," *Dictionnaire biographique des frères prêcheurs*, https://dominicains.revues.org/85.

His main contribution came at the very outset of the council. He and other like-minded theologians were troubled by the preliminary schemas drawn up by the Preparatory Commissions, worrying that their defensive, rigid tenor and exclusive emphasis on ecclesial authority betrayed the tone of openness the pope had established in calling for the council. Chenu and Karl Rahner corresponded about their mutual fear that these schemas threatened to stymie the potential for renewal before the council even began. Chenu mused that a brief text addressed from the council fathers to the outside world, prior to any major doctrinal deliberations, might set a better course. He eventually took it upon himself to draft such a document, which Congar circulated among the French bishops, with Chenu's name removed to protect the document from the contagion of his tainted reputation.[30] A heavily edited version of this text would indeed go on to become the council's first published text, the Message to the World, signaling the church's willingness to engage beyond its own confines. Chenu's initiative succeeded, although he did lament that the edits deeply changed the content and tone of his original draft. As he put it, "They drowned my kid in holy water!"[31]

Chenu was also invited to serve on the "signs of the times" subcommission for Schema XIII, which would later become *Gaudium et Spes*. His socially engaged theology had an eye on the "signs of the times" before the phrase gained momentum at the council, so he was well positioned to promote this notion during the council. As intense debate brewed over Schema XIII, splintering the erstwhile united German and French majority of council fathers, Chenu became an enthusiastic advocate for the phrase. In October 1965, he gave a robust defense of the Ariccia draft of Schema XIII in a speech at the Centro di Documentazione Olandese,[32] and then once the document had passed, he wrote extensively about the theological value of "the signs of the times" in the postconciliar era.[33]

30. For more detail, see Chenu, *Vatican II Notebook: A Council Journal, 1962–1963*, trans. Paul Philibert (Adelaide: ATF Press, 2015).

31. Chenu and Duquesne, *Un théologien en liberté*, 178.

32. Published as Chenu, "Une Constitution pastorale de l'Église," in *Peuple de Dieu dans le monde* (Paris: Cerf, 1966).

33. Chenu, "Les Signes des temps," in *Peuple de Dieu dans le monde*, 35–55. Originally published in *Nouvelle Revue Théologique* 87 (1965): 29–39, and Chenu, "Les

Ideas from this period deeply inform his later essays on liturgy. The council became for him a sort of turning point, and his later essays evaluate what the council achieved, and what its reception requires moving forward. It is no wonder that Chenu was a strong advocate for the Pastoral Constitution on the Church in the Modern World, as the notion of church-in-world reflects both the historical consciousness (the world is changing) and social engagement (the church cannot be separate from the world) at the heart of his theological worldview. This commitment is evident in his liturgical theology, in the insistence that to be a human means to be in the world. In his 1974 essay on sacramental anthropology, Chenu repeatedly rejects all dualisms, including that of nature and grace. This *capax dei* vision of the nature/grace relationship, informed by a robust incarnational Christology, suffused his understanding of the "signs of the times" as sites of grace.

While Chenu himself was not a primary actor in the liturgical renewal movement around Vatican II, he resonated with its aims. He shared its methodology of *ressourcement,* returning to older sources for a more capacious understanding of tradition and ritual in the present. We see in his postconciliar writings on liturgy his promotion of and delight in the liturgical developments of the council, which resonated deeply with other conciliar developments in which he played an active role. Vatican II's vision of the church as the people of God, as a church *in* the world, reading and responding to the signs of the times, represented a rehabilitation of Chenu's thought, taking up into the ecclesial mainstream the very notions of historical consciousness and social engagement for which he had been condemned.

After the Council (1965–1990)

Chenu was quite active in the final decades of his life. He embraced and built upon the theologies of Vatican II, especially on questions of the church-world relationship. The inductive theological method he had pioneered earlier in his career intensified during this period. While many of his counterparts lamented the upheaval in both church and society, Chenu saw the liberation movements and rapid social changes

---

Signes des temps: réflexion théologique," in *L'Église dans le monde de ce temps: Constitution pastorale "Gaudium et spes,"* vol. 2 (Paris: Cerf, 1967), 205–25.

of this era as exciting signs of the times, potential sites of grace. Taking the long view of a historian, he argued that rapid social changes and the conflict they catalyze in the church often have corresponded to moments of renewal, like the advent of the mendicant orders in the thirteenth century. Conflict in the church is often, he argued, "proof of a renewal underway."[34]

As a teacher, he continued to encourage students to throw themselves into the realities of their own age, even to the extent of revolutionary social engagement. While his counterpart Henri de Lubac was horrified by the student revolutions of 1968, Chenu was delighted, seeing in them the possibility of grace. Matthew Fox, a student in Chenu's seminar at the Institut Catholique that spring, recalls his seventy-three-year-old professor ending a class by shutting his notebook and announcing, "We have been talking about twelfth-century history—here is your chance to make some history. Go out and join the revolution! Don't come back next week; come back in two weeks and tell me what you have contributed!"[35] His last book-length project, *La Doctrine sociale de l'Église comme idéologie,* promoted this kind of social engagement with the lived realities of the present age, critiquing the notion of "Catholic social doctrine" for its tendency toward deduction and ahistorical abstraction. He advocated instead for a historically contextual, concrete response to social issues that would privilege lived reality as a theological source over abstract, "ideological" systems.[36]

During this time, Chenu developed an interest in Latin American liberation theology in its nascency, embracing notions of liberation, praxis, and base communities. He and Gustavo Gutiérrez seem to have mutually influenced each other; Gutiérrez attributes his decision to become a Dominican later in life as an homage to Chenu's influence.[37] More scholarship is needed to tease out the relationship between lib-

34. Chenu, "Phénomènes de contestation dans l'histoire de l'Église," *Concilium* 68 (1971): 91–96.

35. Matthew Fox, *Confessions: The Making of a Postdenominational Priest,* revised and updated (Berkeley: North Atlantic Books, 2015), 82.

36. Chenu, *La Doctrine sociale de l'Église comme idéologie* (Paris: Cerf, 1979).

37. See Gustavo Gutiérrez, "Befreiungstheologie – eine Tochter Chenus," *Zeitschrift für Missionswissenschaft und Religionswissenschaft* 107 (2023): 249–58.

eration theology and Chenu's earlier work; liturgical praxis could be an important dimension of such a study.

Chenu's collaboration with *petits foyers* continued well into his 90s, inviting laypeople to conversations about the role of women in the church and other such social issues on which he did not publish much, but engaged extensively in informal discussion groups. Until the very end of his life, he was fully immersed in the signs of the times.

Conclusion

While Chenu's primary field was not liturgical theology, his historically conscious, socially engaged theological method had important implications for liturgy, evident in the essays contained in this volume. As an historian in the *ressourcement* movement, as a pastor and theologian committed to worker movements, and as a prelate whose groundbreaking ideas made him the target of censure, his work both shaped and responded to the social, political, and ecclesial happenings of his own time. An appreciation of the intellectual currents, events, and experiences of his lifetime clarifies the significance of his contributions to history, to theology, and to the life of faith.

Part One

Five Articles by Marie-Dominique Chenu

Anthropology and Liturgy (1947)

Para no.

1 For whoever wants to measure the impact of the liturgy in the construction of Christianity, in the economy of the life and the Church's thinking, it is certainly important in the first place to perceive the objective religious quality of its content; but it is also necessary to consider its capacity to express in sacred value the resources and requests of humanity and of the Christian community in prayer. In an economy where the incarnation and the human assumption that it achieves have become the prototype of every Christian act, the truth and the power of a liturgy reside in a "sacramental" regime, i.e., in symbolic sets where grace is expressed and transmitted in human acts ritualized for this purpose. There more than elsewhere, it would be wrong to superimpose the sacred on the profane, or grace on human nature; according to all the realism of effective symbols, it is in itself that this nature is consecrated. The absolute gratuitousness of grace in no way implies the eviction or reduction of the laws and behavior of the human subject; it is this subject which, according to the very intentions of Christ, author of the sacraments, serves as the basis for distributions and symbolic expressions of grace. Thus St. Thomas Aquinas discerns the raison d'être of the seven essential sacraments in the cardinal elements of the personal and collective life of human beings. Therefore, the liturgy will be essentially communal because it expresses the essentially social nature of humanity in the Mystical Body of Christ. Since it assumes the human requests and resources of the Christian community in prayer, the liturgy implies, confirms, and consecrates an anthropology.

2 If this is the case, we can appreciate the importance of a liturgical movement in the life and thought of the Church as well as in the construction of Christianity. At the supernatural level of the sacred, it is the liturgy's task to give an authentic expression to what humanity bears of greatness and misery, of aspiration and truth. It is this movement which will be the most sensitive criterion of a new rooting of grace in evolving humanity, and the guarantor of the difficult balance to be found in this zone of the spirit where God comes to live. At the same time, one can imagine, the liturgy finds in this science of humanity its openness to the current world, as well as its capacity to sacramentalize in its "ceremonies" certain activities typical of contemporary human beings. Pastoral therefore by definition, it is nourished by tradition, both divine tradition and valuable human traditions, without giving in to archeologism.

3 Let us analyze the benefits of such a precious coherence.

4 The liturgy brings about the encounter, and thereupon the equilibrium of the supra-rational and the infra-rational, the conjunction of which constitutes the privileged psychological nature of the sacred, its connatural atmosphere. Let us now put some Christian terms on this psychoanalytic vocabulary: the liturgy is accomplished in a conjunction of the mystery (supra-rational)[1] and the symbol (infra-rational), two human powers so difficult to regulate, that we are often tempted to recast them for the benefit of a pure rational balance, either intellectualism in theology, or formalism in the liturgy or in any other discipline. This happens especially where, in action as in thought, the transmission of capital seems threatened by this mysterious element and by this symbolic element, whose double behavior cannot be accommodated solely by the forms of reason and the established order.

5 The human person, spirit in a body, consubstantially united with a body, does not perform any act which does not find its

1. The word is obviously taken here not in the sense of a revealed truth, possibly formulated in a dogma, but in the sense of a sacred action, containing, in some way, grace.

soil and its organic sap in the infra-rational zone of itself, where it is, near the material world, the unity of the biological and the psychological. In the same way, the human being will ensure the fullness of their action only by going beyond rational calculation and conceptual and prudential analysis, to flourish at the mysterious and harmonious summit of their spirit. The human person, being human in and by reason, is only entirely master of themself there, and ends up in the worst disorders when they renounce this mastery and gives themself up to the seductive and scabrous forces which attract it above or below, from the biological instinct to the intuitions of genius. Rational discernment and critical thinking are always and everywhere the indispensable rule of thought and action, even in the domain of the sacred.

6 But the domain of the sacred, more than any other, cannot be enclosed in the rational forms of the mind. It overflows on all sides while crossing them and integrating them unceasingly, until its communion with the divine is accomplished. Balance is very difficult to maintain, because here the fieriest thrusts of the religious powers of humanity are exerted, in an anxious dialectic where the purity of the mind is claimed even as the most vivid imagery of the senses is brought into play. This balance of the Church of Christ in the history of its spirituality is not the least testimony to its truth.

7 Yet the liturgy provides the Church with this delicate discipline of the irrational on the proper territory of the sacred: the mystery and its cultic expression in symbolic elements. More than ever, we can measure the scope of such a resource: the primary trait of the new humanity that we see born in this twentieth century, in extravagant outbursts, is the violent growth of these irrational elements, either supra- or infra-rational. Savage anti-intellectualism, the political and social effects of which are revealed as the harmful consequences of the excesses of thought. But these excesses must not compromise the healthy reaction they manifest against rationalism which, since the "natural theology" of the eighteenth century, and even since Descartes, had rejected its symbolic and mystical elements to the margins of the sacred. This long and sad story suffices to evoke and denounce the origins of the liturgical failure of a certain Christianity.

8 Here are restored, in Christendom as in humanity, these magnificent powers, in the unity of the human composite, subject of grace, in the community of the Christian people in prayer, accessible to the rhythm of collective life, even to its relationship with God. Symbolic acts in which the mystery of Christ is expressed and embodied in his Mystical Body. These are magnificent but also formidable powers which the infallible Church captures and saves in the discipline of her liturgy. The severe criticism that we must make, with Professor De Greef,[2] of these instinctive forces of the body, the imagination and the spirit, cannot and must not exclude, among the leaders of a liturgical movement, the doctrinal and practical problems posed by the liturgy's right to be based on these human mechanisms whose spiritual content is, in the philosophical sense of the word, equivocal, on these fragile and at the same time necessary values. To what extent are these values oriented and qualified by what is supernatural truth in the liturgy? How will this truth actually have enough force, liturgically, and not only morally, to exploit, in the spirit of the divine sacraments of Christ, these infra- and supra-rational resources of the new humanity for the Christianity of tomorrow?

9 There can be no question of analyzing the content of these irrational elements here; a cursory consideration of the liturgical life allows us to recognize that they are like the ground on which the liturgy must work.

10 First, the liturgy is presented as a series of actions, not as the conceptual development of a theory: sacramental, sacrificial, and latreutic actions, which involve a concrete commitment on the part of the whole person. They are certainly charged not only with spiritual values, but precisely with intellectual content, with ideas, and with truth; however in the form and in the living flesh of sacred acts, where the gesture comprises unconscious and ineffable riches.

11 These actions are symbolic, that is, their material gesture—from the consecrating act to the garment's color—is ordered, organized,

2. Translators' note: Chenu does not specify, but it seems not unlikely that he is referring here to the work of Guillaume De Greef (1842–1924), a Belgian sociologist who was strongly influenced by Auguste Comte.

transformed by representing a spiritual, mysterious, intrinsically sacred reality. Such a relation of matter and spirit is not made of abstract signs, abstractly analyzable and rationally arranged; the meaning plays out in a realistic, almost crude image (a bath, a meal) which ought not to be minimized under the guise of spiritualizing or intellectualizing it. May it keep its indefinable plasticity and this heady richness where intellectual tenuity does not limit affectionate perception. Vehicle of mystery, so silly and so suggestive at the same time. The faithful no longer learn their catechism: they are "initiated."

12 Finally, these symbolic actions appear, develop, and multiply in collective bodies: communities of the Christian people where the participants are actors and not just spectators. They are therefore tuned to the modes and means of this original knowledge that every social psychology observes in groups, where almost instinctive exchanges compose a powerful climate, irreducible to anyone's gibberish.

13 Such is, at the heart of the liturgy, the Eucharistic meal: a meal, therefore an action, a symbolic action, accomplished in common. An understanding which would escape from these contexts to express itself would ruin the very intelligibility to which it aspires. A whole pedagogy is included there, perfectly suited in principle to the knowledge of mystery, of which the symbol is the most human expression. Our contemporaries are certainly more disposed to it than the rationalists of the eighteenth century.

14 Symbol and mystery: these two essential pivots of the liturgy, body and soul of sacramental life, are in fact linked to each other, in a reciprocal request and as in a mutual safeguard. The one cannot be taken out without devaluing the other.[3] An infra-rational value,

3. Against this devitalization of both, provoked by a unilateral anti-Protestant apologetics, contemporary theology has rightly reacted in recent times, not without connection with the anti-rationalist reaction that we observed in human understanding. The notion of the sacrament as mystery has come back into circulation. We must therefore avoid blurring the value of signification, while situating it in the complex whole of the sacramental economy: the sacrament is both sign and symbol, sign and mystery. Cf. the excellent theological balance presented by Fr. Roguet in the notes accompanying his translation of St. Thomas's *Summa*.

the symbol obviously does not have the firmness, the lucidity, or the stability of concept, and it will one day have to be guaranteed by a homogeneous conceptual statement: fine work for the theologian. But this necessary operation must not treat the symbol as being of inferior quality, nor conceal its high religious power, nor distort its original dialectic. The symbol does not develop and cannot be trained according to the rules of conceptual knowledge; it proliferates by a kind of imaginative contamination of its matter, and as long as it retains its point where it is expressly the "type" of the mystery, its growth is organic and beneficial. This polarization of the mystery makes it, down to its detail, a spiritual nourishment of faith, which, as an intellectual act and act of adhesion, is nourished here by tasty representations. *Lex orandi, lex credendi.* Thus, the sacrament develops according to multiple representations, from which we have moreover very fruitfully identified the play and intelligibility by arranging them on three levels: memory of the past actions of Christ, effective representation of present grace, and pledge of future bliss. But this conceptualization must respect the resistance which, in a religious aura, the symbolic representation of the mystery opposes to it.[4]

Lex orandi, lex credendi. The famous axiom does not bear only on the objective content of collective prayer, of which the positive theologian collects the testimony among the Church Fathers, doctors, pastors, and mystics; it also signifies, even more profoundly, that the internal law of faith (*lex credendi*), its working method, is related to the internal law of prayer in a spiritual economy whose structures are constituted by symbolic actions. A faith which, in order to better formulate itself, would consider these modes of expression as rudimentary and superficial, would impoverish the soil from which, in part, it draws its sap.

See Thomas d'Aquin, *Somme Théologique: Les Sacrements IIIa Qu. 60–65,* ed. Aimon-Marie Roguet, Éditions de la revue des jeunes (Paris: Cerf, 1999 [1945]).

4. So with the multiple elements of the symbolism of water in baptism. Or, with more subtlety, the appropriateness of the multiple rites of the eucharistic celebration analyzed by Thomas Aquinas, *Summa Theologiae* IIIa, q. 83, a. 5.

16 Metaphor and symbol have something floating, equivocal; this is why, from the outset, the liturgy determines the symbolic "matter" by a "form," a statement which fixes the point of the symbol. It is, however, the matter which remains the living flesh of sacramentalism. It is distressing to see how too often it is brought back to pseudo-philosophical categories, where, by an undue transfer of Aristotelian hylomorphism, the pre-theological character of the symbolic game is eliminated.

17 Sometimes it is liturgists themselves who have sinned. Periodically, in history, the temptation is to allegorize, that is to say to submit the symbol to an analysis which conceptualizes its dissociated elements. The paschal candle is the figure of the Risen Christ: what a copious image! But, in a candle, there is the wax, the wick, the flame: the wax is humanity; the wick is the divinity; the flame is the Spirit, etc. This is displaced intellectualization, which evacuates both the fundamental meaning of the symbol and its religious power. It also includes an aristocratic refinement which detaches primitive perception from its popular soil and deprives it of its permanent youth. Our liturgy preserves, alas, too many traces of clumsiness.[5]

18 The liturgy, the mysterious presence of God through the intermediary of symbols, is the vital environment in which the primitive religious powers of human beings find their balance. It is also, in the positive revelation of Christ, the vital environment in which faith can develop rationally, without reducing the irrational elements of its "initiation." *Lex credendi.*

19 Second reflection, which we will present again in the form of a dialectic between two spiritual densities to be maintained in communion: the liturgy achieves the balance between the individual and the group, or more precisely it provides the person with the community ground necessary for the promotion of grace.

5. We do not at all mean by this to condemn the use of allegory: it has its place in the liturgy as in the literary genres of the Bible. It is the allegorization of elements whose intrinsic value is symbolic that we reject. Both the symbol and the mystery suffer as a result.

20 There is no question of evoking the outdated debate between the liturgists and the supporters of private prayer. It is a question here, on the religious level, of the general problem of the role of the community in the development of the person. We know well enough how this perennial problem finds itself today, at all levels, at the very center of the revolutionary context. The economic solidarities which now seize us, on the spot, and from one end of the universe to the other, the expansion of human activities by the elimination of distances and the speed of exchanges, the concentration of companies, the socialization of labor, the organization of professions, the ideological power of information and propaganda, the diffuse feeling of the coherence of a humanity on the march in the midst of the worst tragedies: so many constitutive elements of a mass civilization, of which we first feel the heavy weight, but of which we must not underestimate the greatness and the benefits, even spiritual ones. In any case, it poses the problem of the relationship between the person and the community, or better still, of the various communities in which the person is involved.

21 This community revolution is obviously refracted on the territory of Christendom, either because grace there assumes these human powers and these new values, or because the community of the Mystical Body is itself seized by a similar aspiration. Yet it is not only on the apostolic level of evangelization and on the administrative level of the parishes that the renewal is manifested; it is in this essential expression of the Christian community that sacramental acts with their collective rites are found. So that, faced with these secular "liturgies" aroused by mass ideologies and totalitarian regimes, Christians feel the concern to capture these community instincts for the benefit of the communion of salvation in which they live. It is in this atmosphere that the liturgical renewal develops.[6]

6. P. Reuter presented this perspective with the required discretion to the first liturgy days at Vanves; see "Des liturgies laïques modernes au renouveau de la liturgie chrétienne," in *Études de pastorale liturgique*, ed. Pie Duployé and Aimon-Marie Roguet, Lex Orandi 1 (Paris: Cerf, 1944), 187–211. For a more technical study, on the basis of traditional theological data, see also Jean Travers, *Valeur sociale de la liturgie d'après saint Thomas d'Aquin*, Lex Orandi 5 (Paris: Cerf, 1947).

22 But the sociological parallelism that we thus observe immediately manifests both the originality of the Christian position and the difficulty of the balance that it requires. For, in Christianity, it is the person who is the subject of grace, in a love of God which, like all love, is incommunicably personal, in a faith which is the supreme act of inviolable freedom. A member of a Mystical Body of which Christ is the head, the person keeps their autonomy there, carries their own sins and merits there, speaks secretly to God, believes and loves towards and against all. This is the opposite of the depersonalization of the masses and the domination of collective instincts, however pious.[7]

23 And yet, this religious exaltation of the person is realized only in the regime, the rhythm, and the fusions of the community, not only of the mysterious community of the Body of Christ, but in the fraternal community which translates it meaningfully. It is even there that the small Christian people, this first client of the Gospel, finds the necessary resources for their life. Even more, it discovers the communal quality of the sacrament more spontaneously than the patent devotee; it is this people who has the greatest need to take an active part in the sacrificial meal; to treat baptism as an entry into the community, to take up the gestures and confessions of the first Christians' collective penance. The testimonies of the laity of the Paris Mission, such as those we heard with emotion from the first liturgical days of the CPL (Vanves, 1944),[8] are revealing; and we are extremely struck by the way in which the most advanced apostles of the people promote the liturgical shapes of their Christianity under construction, against the hardening and routines of the past. There could be no better sign of good Christian health. The community is the necessary place for Christian life, for the promotion of people in grace as in nature. Liturgical truth covers human truth. Let the liturgists take notice.

24 The liturgy will therefore be reborn in proportion to the rebirth of true communities. All the sociology of communities operates on this sacred ground as it does on secular grounds: it will be

7. Cf. the work of Professor De Greef, to which we have already alluded. Translators' note: see our comments on the identity of De Greef above.

8. Translators' note: i.e., the Centre de Pastorale Liturgique.

necessary to observe the laws and the techniques, starting with a detection of the natural communities (of neighborhood, of work, even of leisure) which will be, against the leveling of the masses, the protection of people, or against the neutralization of sluggish parishes, the spring of an active liturgy.[9] Liturgical pastoral care has great and beautiful tasks ahead of it.

25 Of the many analyses and perspectives that present themselves, we will only retain one by way of example to propose an important discernment, supported moreover by general observations of sociology. It is necessary to distinguish among the communities what I will call the cell-communities and the meeting-communities. The cell-communities are those which have a permanent value in the constitutive fabric of the society. The prototype is based on the family as an elementary unit, the grouping of homes: a group of cells homogeneous by way of life, preoccupations, the same demands of love, and the same sacramental grace. The close intimacy which spontaneously arises from these common goods effectively achieves a fraternity worthy of the first Christian communities, and, spontaneously again, the collective gestures of the primitive Churches are reborn there, from spoken prayer to common penance. It is on this type, we believe, that the parish will be built, the true parish, a territorial community where the family (with a man being considered as a husband and a father, not as a worker) finds the place of sanctification of its essential works.[10]

26 The meeting-communities respond to completely different needs: temporary communities, of intense density and fervor, they respond in a Christian manner to these great gatherings which the twentieth century saw multiply in social life. The people there obviously have a different behavior than in the cell-communities. The liturgy will be different, both in content and in dynamic. The

9. We are thinking of such a Parisian parish where a federation of base communities is in the process of regrouping, of reincarnating this amorphous mass which is inevitably with a "parish" of 50,000 inhabitants.

10. Needless to say, the major interest of the experiences of Michonneau in Colombes, of Father Loew in Marseille (neighborhood community, basis of "parish" life), etc.

occasions as well as the modalities will significantly vary; recent achievements (Congress of the JOC in 1936,[11] Night of the Parisian Parishes at the Colombes stadium in 1946) have shown us the delicate conditions of such gatherings and demonstrated their religious power. They can certainly include whole blocks of ordinary liturgy, but their overall organization requires, in liturgy and paraliturgy, a kind of creative imagination charged with expressing the collective emotion of the moment on a traditional basis. The joy of the people in thanksgiving at Colombes will be expressed admirably in the dancing of the Alleluia. Replicating the sacred level of mass phenomena, they will be an essential element in a Christianity commensurate with the new world. The experiences already authorize a firm hope.

27 We will add with Fr Bouyer that,[12] whatever these community rites might be, they are first and foremost the internal expression of Christian communities as such; the liturgy is there for itself and is not in itself a direct means of apostolate. But by this very fact and through this specific fidelity, there is an admirable power of expansion, whether in the intimacy of the cell-communities, or in the contagion of meetings. A perfection, moreover, which gives these communities a high quality of conquest in a pagan world.

28 Third consideration: the liturgy achieves the balance between inspiration and discipline. We will confine ourselves to a few considerations of principle about this difficult problem.

29 It is a common place to praise the eminent value of the liturgy, especially of the Roman rite, in the education and disciplining of religious feelings. No need to repeat that here. Perhaps even the insistence was sometimes one-sided and caused some bad humor

11. Translators' note: that is, the Young Christian Workers movement (the *Jeunesse ouvrière chrétienne*) founded by Cardinal Cardijn in 1925. Mary Kate Holman discusses Chenu's connections to this movement in her chapter in this volume.

12. Translators' note: that is, Louis Bouyer. Chenu does not specify a precise source he is referring to here.

as a reaction. We believe that the liturgy maintains the resources of inspiration even in its divinely stable forms.

30 Let us note immediately that under this word of inspiration it is not a question of the pious initiatives and fantasies of each, but of the inspiration of Christian communities, formed in a hierarchical Church. Each person is free in their private prayer, but, in public worship, they have to surrender to the discipline of the community and obey the hierarchical priesthood.

31 In addition, this inspiration can find its impetus and authenticity only around the essential acts of worship, such as instituted by Christ and preserved by his Church. A zone even surrounds them, which without being of divine institution, holds a permanent value of truth and construction. For example, the canon of the mass.

32 But this very example, at the heart of the liturgy, introduces us to an area where already, throughout history, inspirations have played differently. The diversity of rites, to which the Church holds so firmly, extends to this traditional domain.

33 History is here a qualified counsellor—"a theological locus"—showing us the role of inspiration, thus understood, in the development of the liturgy. St. Pius V's deadlock in the face of the violence of the Lutheran Reformation cannot prevent us from benefiting from these lessons of history, even at the expense of the rubricists. The intelligibility of rites is in fact very permeable to requests and initiatives of an inspiration which is otherwise subject to the current discipline. Formerly the desire to see the host, which was the most lively sensation of the real presence (in the thirteenth century), more recently communion considered as normal participation in mass, or even certain requests of the Catholic Action and missionary apostolate, are all examples of the scope of which we have rightly underlined: lofty inspirations, drawn from the heart of the surest sacramental truth, which were sponsored by the competent ecclesial authority. Martimort drew the curve of a liturgical evolution where inspiration and discipline are the components of a well-ordered economy.[13]

13. Aimé-Georges Martimort, "L'histoire et le problème liturgique contemporain," in *Études de pastorale liturgique*, ed. Duployé and Roguet, Lex Orandi 1 (Paris: Cerf, 1944), 97–126.

34 We will reach the causes and find the measure of this economy by observing the tension which develops, in the liturgical life, between the symbol and the rite. The symbol possesses an effervescent power always at work; the rite fixes the material, the forms and the gestures of this symbol. The symbol is mouldable under the presence of the mystery it represents; the rite socially guarantees the truth of this presence. Not even the fixation and respect for words in outdated languages do not find there, *servatis servandis,* their raison d'être, in a necessary ritualism. The daily experience of the Church regulates this balance, which is variously assured according to the articulations of the sacramental organism.

35 One will have noted how the elements that we have observed and classified under these three headings overlap: symbolic and mystical values in the face of institutional and conceptual formalisms, education of people in an essentially communal regime, and the role of inspiration in the discipline of rites. The laws of the sacred, which ratify and consecrate the Christian economy, become intelligible to us in the very nature of humanity, the subject of grace; and the circumstances that the human being is going through illustrate its significance before our eyes.

36 Of course, the Church is not only a society of worship, but also a communion in faith, hope, and charity. If, however, a Christianity is built not only by the moralization of human life, but above all by the sacramentalization of some of its essential acts which have become constitutive of the Mystical Body of Christ, it is clear that the liturgy will be the mysterious and visible expression of this Christianity, and at the same time, the criterion of its divine and human truth.

The Sacraments in the Christian Economy (1952)

Para no.

1 If we had questioned, thirty years ago, a professor of theology or a catechist on the place of the sacraments in the Christian economy, both, each at their educational level, would have commented on the thesis *De necessitate sacramentorum*: God carries out the salvation of humanity according to the very condition of human nature and according to the concrete states of this nature, thus bringing remedy and life to the very place where failure and death have been inserted. A great classical thesis, where theological reflection emanates directly from the observation of God's effective action in God's work of redemption. But, in fact, this thesis would have been developed within an abstract consideration of humanity, without any concern to detect the temporal articulations of this divine behavior, evoking only in the margin, and for the record, the possible or real variations in sacramental functions. Thus the ample developments of the Church Fathers in their catecheses, and the masters of the Middle Ages in their Summas—devoted to the "ceremonies of the Old Testament," the prefigurations of each of the rites, the triple temporal symbolism of the sacraments, etc.—would have remained atrophied. Moreover, by the erasure of this last point, a certain realism of sacramental efficacy would have seriously affected the exact balance of the "presence" of a mystery both past and future, and aroused, above all for the sacrifice of the mass, some theory of re-production that the theologies of the seventeenth and eighteenth centuries constructed, in ignorance of sacramental symbolism. In short, the historical and temporal

element included in the structure of the mystery and the Christian rite would more or less consciously have faded away.

2 Today, the massive, and almost violent, irruption of two spiritual factors has imposed the reclassification and re-balancing of several elements of the Christian sacrament: on the one hand, the reinvigoration of the notion of a Christianity conceived as an "economy" (and the renewed reading of the Eastern Fathers feeds this awakening); on the other hand, the acute awareness of time as a necessary dimension of human conduct, including on the spiritual and religious level. The theme of this session captures these two resources, the secular and the Christian, whose homogeneity is immediately understood. Here we are in the very core of our reflection: pastoral ministry and liturgy emanate from an "economy" of salvation. We thus grasp the density of such contributions, as we feel the urgency of carefully defining their balance, both for an orthodoxy of truth and for an effective pastoral practice.

3 Before organizing the elements of this reconstruction, and to place these two terms of *sacrament* and *economy* in their proper context, let us quickly lead our analysis to the point where the problem will arise. We will only give the outline of these approaches, since they are preliminary to the main subject. The other reports of this session also support the picture.

4 Christianity *is* an economy of salvation: such is the fact and truth of revelation, in the total sense. Not only a teaching of truths, but, thanks to this teaching, the transmission of the divine life to humanity according to the steps arranged by God. Participation in being, therefore, and not only indoctrination. Of course, doctrine is the basis, criterion, and key to this participation, for this participation is done by and in the "Word of God." But this Word of God, following its course, is consumed in an incarnation: the Word becomes flesh, at the center of this divine history, and this event impacts the time before and the time after, at the same time as it fixes the authentic regime of the divine life in humanity.

5 What is, then, the economy of salvation? Two concepts manifest the framework, both in their content and in their conjunction: the economy is both mystery and history, that is to say mystery in history, and history in the mystery of Christ. This link is all the more

striking in that the elements involved are seemingly contradictory. Mystery: understood obviously not as the statement of a transcendent truth, but, in the objective sense, the very transcendent reality of this divine life, as given entirely gratuitously to human beings to participate in. History: this means that this gift is made according to a preparation, an unfolding, a fulfillment, in temporal forms which are not the accidental episodes of an abstract operation, but the internal steps of an economy in tune with human time.[1]

6 The Bible describes how this mystery is unfolded in history. God does not write a book (which I would read), but a story (in which God engages, and I with God). The liturgy is the extension of this story, its perfection, in figure and in reality. We all agree here on this connection between the Bible and the liturgy: it is in this consubstantiality that the liturgy is defined.

7 How does the liturgy realize this? By a re-presentation (not a re-production) of the mystery, which, accomplished once and for all, is nevertheless present today and in all times. This is the "sacrament." The economy is necessarily sacramental. It is so not only because of seven rites, isolated actions, vaguely collective practices, but because of an organic set of words, gestures, songs, prayers, celebrations, which participate both in virtue of and in the actual expression of the mystery, and which composes an immense sacramental reality, from which flows forth the Church's deepest life, at the same time as the entire universe offers it its material.

8 The sacraments are therefore ritual actions by which we are united to the mystery in history, and united, in the mystery, to the history of Christ, God incarnate, incorporating humanity. The sacramental order is in physical continuity with the economy of mystery.

9 Here we work to analyze the structure of the sacraments, better still, of sacramentality as a whole. The edge of this sacramentality is symbolism: the sacrament is a symbolic action, which is both

1. "The Christian mystery was not delivered to us in a series of timeless definitions, unrelated to any precise historical situation, even if this meant allowing itself to assume whatever biblical images we wished later on, by way of illustration." Henri de Lubac, *History and Spirit: The Understanding of Scripture according to Origen* (San Francisco: Ignatius Press, 2007), 433.

the appropriate mode of the representation of the mystery (and of the mysteries), and the presence in time of this mystery.

10 A central notion, as Tradition moreover testifies, which cannot be offset by the polemical and unilateral concern of a counter-Reformation theology. At this moment when, going beyond polemical contexts, we are becoming more aware of the sacramental organism, it is supremely important to work out, in the very structure of the Church, this link between the sacrament and the economy of salvation: the sacrament leads us to an understanding of the economy, at the same time that a more acute sense of the economy establishes sacramental and liturgical renewal on its deep soil.

Mystery and Symbolism

11 Each time that a knot is reached, in thought as in action, the analysis which must untie it is particularly disappointing, because its abstraction sets aside in advance the very crossing of the threads, in order to be able to follow the texture of each thread. We must, however, give in to this necessary abstraction; at least let us take care to observe, at each step, the constant interference of the threads which are tied and find their own consistency in this very knot.[2]

12 First thread: the mystery calls for the sacrament. What does this connection consist of? The symbolic operation is not only a literal or gestural figure, covering a hidden reality from the outside by an imaginative artifice; it is the proper means of expressing a mysterious reality in literary and cultic terms (so, by means of an act), thanks to the distant gap between two realities, of which one is able, in some way, to represent the other. We are situated in front of an admirable resource of the spirit, which, in its order and accord-

2. Focusing explicitly on the organic arrangement of the concepts and themes in question, we will refrain from giving bibliographical references or entering into discussions, here inappropriate, for each of the elements of the construction. Readers can easily refer to the publications and works in progress ([Anscar] Vonier, [Odo] Casel, [Oscar] Cullmann, [Josef] Jungmann, etc.), without forgetting the controversies provoked in Germany by the liturgical renewal.

ing to the authenticity of its line, is as great and as fruitful as this other understanding which, reaching things in their causes, obtains knowledge of them. The explanation of science and the meaning of the symbol: two types of heterogeneous knowledge, in themselves at least, whose processes and values must in no way destroy each other, if we know how to determine their field and methods.

13 The measure of the symbolic value is taken from the distance between the thing-sign and the reality-mystery, from the hiatus experienced between the two, and which imposes a leap from the visible material thing to a certain profound density which will provoke the transfer to the hidden reality. An exhilarating rise, charged with affectivity, which can only be accomplished in and by an "initiation," and not by indoctrination (of the type of science, for the most part). Poetic power, to the point that a liturgy which is not born poetically, is a failure. Power of exaltation also, which bursts with joy, and, so to speak, relieves itself in the feast. The symbol is not an ornamental accessory of the mystery, nor a provisional pedagogy; it is the co-essential resource of its communication. Such is the depth of a psychological and ontological insertion of the rite, of the ritual symbol, into the mystery. Such is the bond of mystery and symbol.

14 This is, of course, traditional doctrine, and also, even more fundamentally, traditional conduct in the Church, and, from before the Church, in all the stages of revelation. It must be recognized, however, that Western theologies of the sacrament-sign have somewhat narrowed the scope of such a conception. The Augustinian analysis of the sign provided sacramental theology with an admirable middle ground for elaboration; but to the extent that it set aside or reduced the content of the mystery-sacrament, as still expressed by the Isidorian definition of the *sacramentum sacrum secretum*, it imposed options for the systematic interpretation of the Christian sacrament, to the detriment of its total equilibrium.

15 The spiritual density of symbolic expression is absolutely original and irreducible to conceptual expression, precisely because its mode of referring to the mysterious transcendent is original. The concept, as we know, can be stretched by the process of analogy, and this is undoubtedly the most beautiful theological

operation there is; still it is the case that this desperate attempt of human intelligence and the "science" of God cannot discredit nor eliminate the symbolic process, which rests precisely on the insurmountable distance between two realities, the sensible and the mysterious, whereas the concept wants to express its relative continuity. Also, the concept congenitally expresses relations of causality; here again, even if they overlap, we are confronted with relations of another order, relations of signification.

16 This does not mean that we should give up conceptualizing symbols. Never should the human person, even in the immersion of the connatural ways of sensitive imagery, renounce the resources of intelligence and its rational procedures. But this elevated labor of the theologian will have to be accomplished in the mystery, and therefore in the contexts and in the climate of symbolism which contain and deliver it. And of course, in the same way and for the same reasons, this applies to catechetical teaching.

17 The elaboration of symbols is done normally and spontaneously by an allegorization of their content. The liturgists know well enough which determinism has pushed not only the professional interpreters of rites, but also the most candid practitioners, the "faithful," to develop literary and cultic symbols into allegorizing expressions. The liturgists also know what threat this slope of intelligibility and ritual observance conceals. However, we must first recognize its authentic value, which is moreover revealed by the history of all religions: allegory is a means of interiorizing, of spiritualizing ritual gestures, even if they are purely self-utilizing, in connecting them one by one, and piece by piece, to the play and the dynamism of the symbolic whole. Texts and rites of Easter find intelligibility and efficacy in the typology of the Exodus. The unleavened nature of consecrated bread is much more than a rubrical respect for the memory of the ancient custom—however without any significance today—of unleavened bread. But the limits of such a process are very narrow, because the construction of the allegory is quite different from the internal rhythm of the symbol. This second-degree operation tends to remove the very matter of the symbol, at the end of which the rite becomes a rebus handed over to archaeologists; it also tends to evacuate the mystery, to

substitute for it an esoteric doctrine and gesture. The literalism of the symbol, its naturism, if I may say so, is the best guarantee of its value and its spirit. Beyond this, the liturgy would be nothing more than the repository of pseudosymbols, emptied of human vitality and Christian intelligibility.

18 Especially in this symbol-in-action that is the rite, the mystery, via the symbol, supports, nourishes, vivifies, and, at the opportune hour, recreates the rite, endlessly conferring on it the necessary lyricism in a right composite of words and actions. Such is the Eucharistic banquet, a major case of this perfect coherence. Beyond this, the rite devours the symbol, and only the rubric reigns.

19 Vice versa, the rite contains and preserves the mystery, because the celebration that it objectively structures, beyond the most legitimate sensibilities, thus develops into a healthy and discreet mystagogy.

20 Without further extending these overly concise observations, let us bring together the conclusions in this equation, so traditional in the Christian language, whatever the motives and the variants may have been: *sacramentum* = *mysterium*. Let us say that the "sacramental mystery"—in the mystery of the Church, built of sacraments—is the result of the mystery par excellence, of the mystery revealed over time according to God's plan of salvation for humanity.

21 Here is the second thread of this knot: the mystery in history.

Mystery and History

22 How then is this mystery present in time and in all times? And how are these mysterious symbols planted in history? We feel here the Christian people's aspiration for a permanent youth of the liturgy, and the problem of the Church in history, and the search for a Christian time. In this way, a sacramental theology, which was misled by theories concerning the reproduction of the mystery by the very fact that it ignored the role of time in the economy as well as in human nature, will be put right.

23 We must take into account two things: the mystery was accomplished in time, once, and forever—an evangelical and apostolic

truth excellently highlighted in recent works; but also, this mystery is not today only a simple "memory," to which our faith alone would give spiritual consistency and effectiveness. The mystery is and remains present. But how is this presence accomplished?

24 By way of symbolic action. The symbol is the means of expression of the historical mystery in the continuity of time. It is not an artificial, "spiritual" extension by a kind of fervent imagination: time effectively enters into the fabric of mystery, and the symbolic ritual action is its means. The sacrament is the intermediary between mystery and history; symbolism is embedded in the mystery as much as the mystery is in time. The rite builds this effective symbolism in coordinated actions. Such is the cohesion of symbol and of presence, notably of mysterious presence. The mystery, the mystery of the death and resurrection of Christ, needs the symbol to be present. Hence the law of the spiritual density of the rite: it is all in the realistic vigor of the symbol.

25 Obviously, it is by and in the faith that this law plays, that this coherence is realized. The sacraments are *sacramenta fidei*; by which, precisely, they exist *intra mysterium*. It is here that begins—and we see it started on all sides in a pastoral consciousness in revolt against social and religious conformism—the process of sacramentalism, of a sacramental practice *ex opere operato* without faith, without "mystery"; then the symbol becomes, albeit unconsciously, a magical rite for the minister as well as for the faithful. There is no worse perversion, not only of the practicing subject, but of the whole objective economy whose architecture we have just described. It is literally dismembered.

26 So there is, so to speak, a time of the sacrament, that is to say an unfolding of the mystery in time, thanks to the sacramental meaning. The sacrament signifies at once the past act of the mystery, the presence of grace in the mystery, and its coming fulfillment in the messianic banquet where every figure will disappear. The great medieval theology took pleasure in enunciating in beautiful and dense formulas the incessant developments of patristic catechesis on this point: sacramental symbolism is organized according to this triple reference to the past, to the present, to the future. *O sacrum convivium, in quo . . . recolitur memoria passionis, mens*

impletur gratia, et futurae gloriae nobis pignus datur.[3] Unfortunately, for a long time this great theme only figured in a theology cut off from its liturgical soil, as a vague and pious corollary. It is in truth the basis of the blooming of symbolisms, and it is the needs of this re-presentation that generate, over the centuries, the secondary rites around this essential symbolic triple knot. The rite of the sacrifice of the mass, in its very entanglement, is the illustration of this profound law.

27 However, this sacramental time is constituted by symbolic actions, not by "events," as a secular historian would say. It therefore leaves intact the time of this world, with its proper value. It is up to the theologian to pose and solve the problem of the coherence of history and of the temporal economy of the mystery; with the autonomies that it implies, their distinction will simultaneously ensure salvation's transcendence and presence in the world. We must not make a play on words on the sacramental history/story.[4]

Nature and History

28 So, salvation in the world, or rather, salvation *of* the world. The Christian paradox reverberates here in the sacramental economy and provides us with a new light. Here we are faced with a major fact, on which theology was built: the sacraments find their matter in the elements of the material universe: water, oil, bread, wine, fire, light, etc. Moreover, they are formed by and in typical human gestures: bathing, eating, hand gestures. This mystery, which unfolds like history, does not put itself onto nature, onto the universe, or onto humanity; it is rooted in actions where, from near or far, precisely through and for the constitution of symbols, the whole universe serves as matter. Nature and history meet in the architecture of the same symbol.

3. Translators' note: Chenu is here quoting the Magnificat antiphon for Second Vespers on the feast of Corpus Christi, often attributed to Thomas Aquinas. "O sacred banquet, in which . . . the memory of suffering is recalled, the mind is filled with grace, and a pledge of future glory is given to us."

4. Translators' note: Chenu appears to be urging us to avoid the wordplay possible on *l'histoire* in French, which has the sense both of "story" and of "history."

29 The symbolic architecture will therefore develop on two levels: (i) on the historical level, where the mystery of Christ, of his life, death, and resurrection, is represented by the effective play of words and actions, developing from essential symbolic actions up to allegorical refinements; (ii) on the level of nature, which also has a symbolic dimension, in the water which purifies, in the balm which strengthens, in the meal which restores, rejoices, and creates community, in the fire which lights up, warms, and burns. The tablecloth for the altar will simply be the tablecloth for the meal which covers and adorns the table where we are going to eat: a detail which enlarges, in a healthy representation, the great symbol of the Last Supper. But the tablecloth is also the shroud of Christ in the tomb: an allegorical evocation of the mystery again presaged by the symbolic rite. And so on. If the sacrament is the terrestrial continuation of the mystery, it will be planted in terrestrial matter and in human life, as the history of salvation is planted in human history, without being confused with it, but also without diminishing it. It is, analogically, the same regime of incarnation.

30 When St. Thomas asks himself why there are seven sacraments in the liturgy's collection of rites, he finds an answer and understanding not in the episodes of the transcendent mystery, but in the discernment of seven typical human actions, by which, individually and collectively, the human person organizes their life. At each of these crucial junctures, the gesture which expresses or produces them, bath, meal, conjugal gift, etc., is coupled with a symbolic dimension by which the appropriate grace is conferred at that point. An argument of convenience, of course, with its relativisms as well as with the resources of analysis and contemplation in which the theologian delights. Whatever it is, it supposes that the sacramental order is built according to the needs and undertakings of the earthly human condition. Nature provides, nourishes, and illuminates the symbolic actions of the transcendent mystery.

31 It will therefore be necessary to maintain, both in the understanding of the symbol and in its liturgical practice, the right balance of this double symbolic framework, distinct and so linked at the same time. The Eucharistic meal certainly re-presents the unique sacrifice of Christ; but it realizes this presence in the ges-

tures and customs of a meal, according to daily routine, so prosaic yet so suggestive, of human meals. As St. Thomas observes, all human behavior will be made sacred at the very moment when the unique and irreducible originality of the mystery captures the slightest action for its own benefit. Once again, the naturalism of the symbol, as a whole and in its detail, will be the sign and the guarantor of the good health of its mystical re-presentation. It is not by eliminating the crude rites of the presentation and eating of food that we will better attain spiritual communion with the sacrifice of Christ. The revitalization of the liturgy will only occur through this human realism, up to its current aspirations, as much as through its sense of mystery.

32 At the end of this analysis, we agree with the lesson that was given by Mr. Rauch last year, at the session of Versailles. It concerned the definition of the Christian celebration: "On the one hand, it turns out, to be deeply rooted in worship behavior of human beings of all times: it resorts, in fact, to the means of expression that the human person has always used, to the signs essential to any celebration which are the rites, gestures, words, songs, not even to mention the places, objects, sacred times, nor of the contribution of the arts, crafts and sciences. On the other hand, this Christian celebration achieves a very particular kind of worship; it obeys its own laws, it has its particular structure; for it is based on a revealed given. From this double fact—rooted in human forms of worship, on the one hand; radical dependence on a divine revelation and institution, on the other hand—results an inevitable and inherent tension in any Christian celebration, at all times. Faced with this ever-lively tension, the celebration needs, in each generation, to regain awareness of its originality, so as not to lose or diminish its Christian substance, but also of the authenticity and the human value of its rites and gestures, so as not to compromise their effectiveness."[5]

5. Charles Rauch, "La célébration du culte," *La Maison-Dieu* 20 (1950): 5–6. Translators' note: Chenu is referring to the right pages, but the title of Rauch's contribution is "Sens de la session," opening an issue devoted to "La célébration du culte paroissial" (the celebration of the parish liturgy).

33 The Christian celebration is therefore the exact emanation of the economy of salvation: the sacramental symbolism which constitutes it is the appropriate expression of the mystery, in the continual representation in history, and in making earthly and human realities a suitable material to signify and to bear the various resources of divine life, according to the institution of Christ and of his Church. The liturgy finds its light there, and pastoral ministry the rule of its efficacy.

Faith and Sacrament (1962)

Para no.

1 Once again, the return to the sources, to the living sources of the Word of God, leads us to rebalance and revitalize theology, the mature understanding of this Word. This time, the renewal of catechesis, with the admirable conjunction of the missionary movement and the liturgical movement—a double awakening of the Word of God, in itself and in its cultic continuity—imposes on us a more organic theology of faith and sacrament, of faith *in* the sacramental structure, and of the *sacramenta fidei*, as the master theologians of the thirteenth century said in a very formal language.

2 Certainly, the theologians had not failed to keep the close connection between faith and the sacrament, according to the most explicit affirmation of the revealed given. But, sometimes under the pressure of the situation and its polemics, sometimes by an intellectualism which did not safeguard the concrete unity of the sacramental action in a difficult conceptual framework, they were not always able to give an adequate expression, in the mystery, to the cultic commitment of faith. We will note the sad admission made, some fifteen years ago, at the very moment when the awareness of the liturgical movement and of the missionary movement started to express themselves, by a theologian well-versed in doctrine and pedagogy: "Is baptism still the sacrament of faith?" This was a title of a very suggestive article by Fr. Dondaine. He said: "Still today, I find it difficult to fix the values (of commitment to faith, as the human side of the sacrament of baptism), to construct

them, to present them to our theology students. We have perhaps a worse perspective than the Fathers."[1]

3 This softening of thinking was reflected in a weakening of the practice of the sacraments, particularly the sacrament of baptism. Or better still, doctrinal weakness recorded the inner distortions of a sacramental whole in which initiation into the mystery was broken down into two operations that had become disparate: a more or less abstract *instruction*, in a "catechism," and a *rite* in which the symbolic and mystical intensities are atrophied by formalism. The de facto separation between the *mystery*, reduced to its theoretical expression, and the *symbol*, reduced to formal signs, disintegrated an operation whose unity guaranteed both the organic structure and the vital dynamism. Both sacrament and faith suffered from this separation. Both, mystery (taught) and symbol (practiced), lost a density that came from their interconnection in what an "initiation" must be. It should be the benefit of the renewal of catechesis to bring together again this unique, vital operation, both in the distribution of its successive acts and in its profound value of *initiation*.

4 It is up to us here to give all its truth—in theological and "theologal" measure[2]—all its resources, its irreducible originality, to catechumenal *initiation*, first by defining theologically the exact coordination of faith and the sacrament, then by manifesting phenomenologically the coherence between mystery and symbol. Thus baptism will manifest itself as the *sacramentum fidei*, in the strong sense that their conjunction gives to these two words, technically and more profoundly. This is to found the catechumenate, in its institution, discipline, and spirit.

5 *Sacramentum fidei*: this, one might say, is the proper name of baptism, of the baptismal mystery lived by the Church in her liturgy. Historians have excellently analyzed, over the past few years,

1. Hyacinthe Dondaine, "Le baptême est-il encore le 'sacrement de la foi'?," *La Maison-Dieu* 6 (1946): 76–87.

2. Translators' note: Chenu is making a distinction here between the adjectives *théologique* and *théologale*. Whereas the first refers to theology as a discipline or field of study, the second refers to the theological virtues of faith, hope, and charity, thereby touching a deeper existential layer.

the emergence and content of the expression, from Tertullian, who put it into circulation, up to the Council of Trent, which canonized it; from St. Augustine, who deepened it in a doctrinal and pastoral context, up to St. Thomas Aquinas, who, nurtured by Augustine, built it in theological rigor.[3] Its erasure, in the textbooks of recent theology, is all the more telling, especially in the doctrinal and pastoral contexts which conditioned it.

6 If *sacramentum fidei* takes on a strong and technical meaning in the language of the Church Fathers and the teachers of the Schools, it is because faith is considered as constitutive of the external sacramental sign, whose whole raison d'être is to manifest a confession of faith. To the extent that the point of application of faith is shifted to the side or beyond the *sacramentum*, i.e., on this side as a disposition, beyond as a use of grace, in order to give the *sacramentum* an absolute and "objective" consistency, we yield more or less to an opposition between faith and baptism, between subjective faith and objective rite; and we come to deal with the dispositions and uses of faith only as a moralist. Fr Dondaine rightly sees in this the weight of the distinction between *opus operatum* and *opus operantis*,[4] thanks to which the Council of Trent teaches the objective efficacy of the sacraments against Lutheranism. But this just and necessary definition of the divine efficacy of the sacrament leaves open the more general problem of the constitution of the sacramental action. Anti-Protestant

3. Cf., in addition to the note of Dondaine, "Le baptême est-il encore le 'sacrement de la foi'?," the major article by Jean Gaillard, "Saint Augustin et les sacrements de la foi," *Revue thomiste* 59, no. 4 (1959): 664–703, in support of his study "Les sacrements de la foi," *Revue thomiste* 59, nos. 1–2 (1959): 5–31, 270–309 (with bibliography); Pierre-Thomas Camelot, "Le baptême, sacrement de la foi," *La Vie Spirituelle* 76 (1947): 820–34; Pierre-Thomas Camelot, "Sacramentum fidei," in *Augustinus Magister* (Paris: Études Augustiniennes, 1954), II:891–96; Pierre-Thomas Camelot, *Spiritualité du baptême*, Lex Orandi 30 (Paris: Cerf, 1960). Finally, several chapters of the masterful work of Edward Schillebeeckx, *De sacramentele heilseconomie* (Antwerp: 't Groeit, 1952), summarized in his *Christ the Sacrament of the Encounter with God* (London: T&T Clark, 2014 [1963]), 65–71.

4. Dondaine, "Le baptême est-il encore le 'sacrement de la foi'?"

polemics must not displace intelligibility beyond the functional balance of the totality of action.

7 Now this action includes, in its very nature as a sign, as a symbol, a reference to the *faith* of the Church. In fact, according to the famous analysis of St. Augustine, it is a compound of two things: a material element (water, bread, oil) and a word, by which this element becomes a symbol of a spiritual reality, an effective sign of divine reality: "*Accedit verbum ad elementum, et fit sacramentum, etiam ipsum tamquam visible verbum.*" The *verbum* is profession of faith: *verbum fidei*. "And whence has water so great an efficacy, as in touching the body to cleanse the soul, save by the operation of the word; and that not because it is uttered, but because it is believed (*non quia dicitur, sed quia creditur*)" (*Tract. in Johannem*, 80, 3). "For the *sacramentum* to be constituted—in other words, for the sign to have its full value as a sign—the element (bread, water, oil) must be accompanied by a word, *verbum*. Thus, this material element is no longer an opaque and unintelligible matter, it takes on a significance and a meaning, it leads the mind to spiritual realities."[5] It is obviously not just any word, but a word having an essential relationship to faith: *faciente verbo, non quia dicitur, sed quia creditur*. "The virtue of this word comes from the fact that it is addressed to the faith of those who use the sacraments and, more profoundly, from the fact that it expresses the faith of the Church."

8 The faith of the Church: for the faith of the faithful who use the sacrament, *fides subjecti* is a human participation in the Church's profession of faith, *fides Ecclesiae*. Thus, the commitment of the person in this testimony of faith takes on an objective value, in the participation in the sacramental celebration. The *protestatio fidei*, which is the living substance of the symbolic act of the Church and—fundamentally—of Christ in and by his Church, is the outward manifestation of spiritual significance, accomplished in an action and in a word, and can only be apprehended by and in the ecclesial faith. "It is in the Church's sacramental . . . confession

5. Pierre-Thomas Camelot, "'Sacramentum.' Notes de théologie augustinienne," *Revue thomiste* 57, no. 3 (1957): 429–49 (441).

of faith of the Church that the risen Christ can make an earthly element or a human act into a sacramentally visible expression of his heavenly act of salvation. . . . In other words, through the sacramental confession of faith human symbolic action becomes the visible prolongation and presence on earth of the invisible saving act of the risen Christ."[6]

9 In the polemic against the Protestants, there has been a certain weakening of the definition of the Council of Trent, which affirms against them that grace is given by the sacrament *ex opere operato*, and not only by faith. To allow the Christological character of the sacraments to fade, they have been treated as "things," having of themselves effectiveness; the *ex opere operato* seemed almost disconnected from the passion and resurrection of Christ. In truth, the sacraments are like the acts and mysteries of Christ (*opus operatum*) which appeal to the faith and commitment of the human being (*opus operantis*): they must in no way seem to be dissociated. *Accedit verbum (fidei)*: the word of faith takes precedence over the "element."

10 Therefore, it is not necessary to use heavily the terms of *form* and *matter*, which for the medieval doctors and—later—for the documents of the Church explain the connection of *word* and *element* as constitutive pieces of the sacrament. Certainly, in its Aristotelian vigor, this terminology is very enlightening: the sacramental sign requires, for its power of expression, that the ritual action be determined by a liturgical formula. A laying on of hands, an anointing or a breath are versatile, and therefore ambiguous, in any case without the essential reference to the work of Christ here in action. The spoken word exerts, on this "matter," a function of "form." But we should not, for the benefit of this fruitful understanding, forget the deeper traditional meaning, according to which the profession of faith "informs" (in the technical sense of the word) the liturgical action, words, and matter. As opportune as it is, the current casuistry on the conditions required for the correct use of matter and form has diverted and still too often

6. Schillebeeckx, *Christ the Sacrament*, 70. See also Gaillard, "Les sacrements de la foi," 24.

diverts attention from the mystical structure of the sacrament, from its true "substance," which was directly aimed at by patristic statements.

11 In order to renew catechesis, it is not a question of unduly exalting the *opus operantis* (the faith of the subject) after having unduly exalted the *opus operatum*, whose objectivism led to the ritual formalism of a sacrament-thing. It is necessary to make conscious and active the union between faith and the sacramentalized act of Christ in the mind of catechumens.

12 This union of principle and structure between faith and the sacramental act is psychologically realized through and in *initiation*. It is crucial to give to this word a strong meaning, that of an operation irreducible to any other, by which only catechesis fulfills its purpose, outside of which one can wonder if it still exists. In truth, initiation is the operation by which faith realizes, through symbolic action, communion with the mystery. The baptized is "one initiated." This is the precondition for faith and the sacrament to be joint.[7]

13 The symbol is the node of this essential conjunction, according to the very nature of the sacrament, and will therefore have to be, according to the extension and variety of its figures in the arrangement of the liturgy, the nourishing soil of catechesis. The symbol is the expression immediately homogeneous to the *mystery*. The concept, the rational statement, the explanation, the definition (provided by the book called "catechism") will later be necessary, but on the condition that they do not devalue the proper and untransmissible intensity of the symbol. *Instruction* must complement *initiation*, but not replace it, or even cover it, if it is true that, in the faith-sacrament conjunction, initiation is a permanent value.

14 The mystery calls for the symbol, that is to say finds in it an expression to its measure in a set of actions and gestures, whose material content, from the basic elements (bath, meal, anointing, laying on of hands, etc.) to the smallest details (color of the gar-

7. The Faith of the Church, ecclesial faith in the act of redemption performed by the Savior, within which the faith of people is expressed. Cf. Schillebeeckx, *Christ the Sacrament*, 65–71.

ment) is commanded, organized, and transformed by the representation of a spiritual and intrinsically sacred reality. The symbolic operation is therefore not only a literal or gestural figure, covering from the outside by an imaginative artifice the hidden reality, the theological or catechetical definition of which would also have been established; it is the proper way to express this mysterious reality in cultic practices.

15 Already at the level of natural knowledge, we are confronted here with an admirable resource of the spirit, which, in its order and according to the authenticity of its development, is as rich and as fruitful as that other understanding which, reaching things in their causes, obtains scientific knowledge about them. The scientific explanation and the meaning of the symbol are two heterogeneous types of knowledge, at least in themselves, whose processes and values must in no way oppose each other, if we know how to determine their scope and methods. How much more is this true in the field of the sacred, the mystery, the Christian mystery, where instruction must be held and developed within initiation.

16 The symbol finds its value and takes its measure in the very distance between the sign-thing and the mystery-reality, in the hiatus experienced between the two, and which imposes like a leap from the visible material thing to a certain deep density that will provoke the transfer to the hidden reality. An exhilarating rise, charged with affectivity, which characterizes initiation, and which would certainly not produce indoctrination. Poetic power, to the point that a liturgy that is not born poetically, is a failure. A power of exaltation too, which bursts forth in joy, and, so to speak, relieves itself in celebration. Not a provisionary pedagogy, but an essential resource of communication. Such is the depth of psychological and ontological integration of the rite (here the ritual symbol) in the mystery. Such is the link of mystery and symbol.

17 Therefore, the symbol is for the initiated more than a simple sign, for which an abstract reference to the signified reality (word, concept) would suffice. Here the reference is carried by the very material of the symbol, in its gravity, I would even say, in its flesh. So let us not "spiritualize" it by premature explanations. Of infrarational value, the symbol obviously does not have the precision,

lucidity, and stability of a concept, and it will one day have to be guaranteed by a conceptual statement; this is the beautiful work of the theologian, already of the catechist, having arrived at the *didascalia*. However, this necessary operation should not treat symbolic sets as inferior, nor as mere preambles. The catechist will very carefully spare the high religious power, will make play the original dialectic. The symbol does not develop and cannot be educated according to the rules of conceptual intelligence; it proliferates by a kind of imaginative contamination of its matter, and as long as it retains its point where it is explicitly the "type" of the mystery, its growth is organic and beneficial. This polarization of the mystery makes it, down to its detail, a spiritual nourishment of faith, which, as an intellectual act and of adhesion, is nourished here by delectable representations. *Lex orandi, lex credendi.*

18 Unfortunately, for several centuries the blocking of the symbolic wholes of baptism into a ritualism of a few minutes, has destroyed their psychological effectiveness, which could not be restored by the best "explanations," because it is the symbol itself that carries its light. The new discipline, by identifying the stages of initiation according to their progressive order, will give the means to let the successive symbols play at the very heart of a liturgy that composes its climate, in a close symbiosis with the successive data of an emerging faith.

19 The use of the categories of "matter" and "form" will thus equally be rejected at the necessary but inferior casuistic level. We have emphasized their value above, together with their patristic origin, but also their specific limit, given their Aristotelian character. It should not be forgotten that these categories were elaborated for the intelligibility of the *nature* of things, of which the internal causes, form and matter, provide the explanation. They are valid to illuminate the *meaning* of these symbolic things, only by comparison: "in the manner of," says St. Thomas (*per modum* formae, *per modum* materiae, he says). The sacramental being is not a "physical" being; it is a sign entirely, in a transfer of its sensitive matter to the hidden reality. Catechesis should not put forward the explanation of these heavy and unsuitable terms in order to preserve their original psychological play in the symbolic acts.

20 A final observation will emphasize the value of the symbol in the sacramental representation of the *Christian* mystery as such. Mystery is accomplished in history, and its symbolic references will have to be assigned first of all by a historical coefficient. The sacraments are the acts of Christ. They therefore contain not only natural symbolism, but a historical reference. The Eucharist is not only a sacred meal, of which religions provide analogues; it is the explicit memory of Christ's last supper close to his sacrifice. Baptism is not only a ritual bath of purification, but the effective representation of Christ's death and resurrection. It is characteristic of the symbol, in its original dialectic, to play at the same time, in its process of meaning, the function of presence and the function of absence: it makes the mystery present, it re-presents the mystery, which was accomplished in the past, and is therefore absent. This is the case maximally in the Eucharistic sacrifice, with its real presence, but also, each in their own way, in every other sacrament, baptism first.

21 Here we are again at the heart of faith in mystery, in what is most realistic, in the sacred "time" of the Church, the Body of Christ. *Opus operatum* in *opus operantis*.[8] What a source of understanding! "The symbol gives rise to thought," says Ricœur, from whom we borrow this analysis, both as a philosopher and as a Christian.[9] *Sacramentum fidei*: yes really, not only in a correct ritual gesture of which faith is a condition, but also in the admirable power of the *intellectus fidei*, to which the simple and the small are "initiated," by the grip of the symbolic wholes, before the *majores* come to theological and catechetical explanations.

8. Translators' note: the original text has *aperantis* here, but this appears to be a typographical error.

9. Paul Ricœur, "Le symbole donne à penser," *Esprit*, July 1959, 60–76. A revised version is included in his book *The Symbolism of Evil* (Boston: Beacon Press, 1969), 347–57.

Anthropology of the Liturgy (1967)

Para no.

1 The human person is the actor in the liturgical celebration. The liturgy finds its subject, its material, its rule, its very being, in humanity. This is trivially obvious. However, upon the slightest reflection, and all the more so in considering the history of the Christian liturgy, or even of religious cults in general, we soon realize that, as often happens, evidence emerges from a global perception that, upon close inspection, turns out to emanate in reality from very complex springs and motives. Discerning these springs and making these motives apparent is an urgent task for the truth and health of the liturgy, especially where it must rediscover its capacity for invention or its creative intuitions, like art or poetry. The time for that has come.

2 Did the Council do it? As we have observed, the Council did not have the benefit of a conscious and elaborated Christian anthropology, neither in the liturgy document nor anywhere else among its texts. The way in which the pre-conciliar projects had been prepared, the agenda delivered to the proceedings of an assembly seized by the *aggiornamento*, and more deeply two or three centuries of a theology out of touch with the human sciences, explain this insufficiency. It is not that a notion of the human being has been ignored or is absent: the deliberations and the texts are filled with fresh and penetrating observations, which color the very style of certain chapters. But there remained implicit—with the notable effectiveness of the consequences—an organic knowledge of the nature, conditions, structures and dynamics of humanity. The Constitution on the Liturgy is a typical case of this position.

It is precisely our task here to bring out those perceptions, both vivid and un-rationalized, which underpin the doctrine and the options taken. An exegesis attentive to the construction of the texts, to the discussions of the commissions, to the amendments adopted or rejected, could suitably give substance to this character of the Constitution. Our goal here is, beyond the texts, and at the service of their intelligibility, to establish the broad lines of this liturgical anthropology. *Homo liturgicus*: the theologian has the capacity to define it, and the joy of considering it.

A Human Liturgy . . .

3 If it is obvious that humanity is the actor of the celebration and that in the history of religions, cults have been the products of temperaments, mentalities, passions and human needs, according to the cycles of civilizations, we also observe that the aspirations and the cultic operations are penetrated and moved by a continuous transfer towards something which transcends human conditions. This is an understandable dynamic, since religion, of itself, is a reference to divinity; but it is also an ambiguous dynamic, since it tends to remove these very human acts from their earthly condition.

4 Leaving to the ethnography of religion the effective analysis of this congenital ambiguity, we will limit ourselves to evoking the whole range of images, attitudes, feelings and exaltations, which manifest this easily dehumanizing transfer among practitioners of the Christian liturgy. It is commonplace in liturgical spirituality to treat our earthly worship as a figure of angelic occupations in paradise. We are associated with the "choirs of angels"; we find there models of adoration, praise, glorification. A healthy theology easily measures the value and the limits of making such comparisons. But there remains, empirically, an eschatological imagery, which penetrates the reflexes, and rapidly the formulas, the gestures, and the devices of worship. The sacred thus implemented is frozen in hierarchy—"angelic"—which decidedly separates the celebrants, clerics and laity, from their usual behavior. Figurative art is the witness of this liturgy. It can also be illustrated, and

guaranteed, by the analogous themes of monastic life considered as an "angelic life."[1]

From another horizon proceeds a similar sublimation, where the liturgy sustains and develops a contemplative life. Since this liturgy is the very "mystery" of Christ represented, made present, in his Body, by symbolic units, it is to be expected that the diversity of accents which can polarize it will be reflected in the fervor of this Christological faith. Concerning the God-Man, some are more sensitive to the human reality of Christ, to his familiar gestures, to his emotions, to his achievements, to his story. They will therefore stay closer to the Gospel stories and will attach themselves to their episodes as to so many objects of contemplation, both in the celebrations of the temporal, from the Nativity to the Passion, and in meditation on the mysteries of the rosary. So they will spontaneously be of the family of doctors of the Antiochene school. Others will see in these episodes and in these traits of humanity only the opportunity to contemplate the Word, thus appeared, in a human nature which is totally assumed by the divine Person. The transfiguration occupies them more than the birth in the manger or the family life at Nazareth. The accounts of the synoptics are overtaken by the Logos of St. John. Like St. Cyril of Alexandria, they are less attentive to the humanization of God in history than to the eternal begetting of the Word and to the "verbification" (*logotheis*) of human beings. Thus, they are led to see in the cultic operation only the support of a contemplation which has their supreme indulgence and which they nourish by the allegorization of vocabularies, images, and rites. Ultimately, they would give in to a kind of liturgical

1. Suso Frank, *Aggelikos bios. Begriffsanalytische und begriffsgeschichtliche Untersuchung zum «engelgleichen Leben» im frühen Mönchtum* (Münster: Aschendorff, 1964). For an accessible presentation, Louis Bouyer, *The Meaning of the Monastic Life* (London: Burns and Oates, 1955), 23–40; Erik Peterson, *The Angels and the Liturgy* (New York: Herder, 1964). St. Jerome, little inclined to these exaltations, quips: "Similitudo promittitur, non natura mutatur" (Likeness is promised, not nature changed), *Epist.* 108, 23.

monophysitism, interiorizing to the extreme the mystery to the detriment of the collective sensibilities of the assembled people.

6 Liturgy, ecclesiology, Christology are homogeneous, in these different theological balances. Catechesis and spirituality are normally experienced in this way, according to the tastes of the Spirit, according to personal or collective charisms, and according to the evolution of cultural contexts. It seems that today, in the theology of the Church in general, and in the theology of the liturgy in particular, it is the God-*Man* who, in Christ, captures the sensibilities of our faith, encouraging a liturgy focused on the history of salvation more than on an allegorizing "speculation."

7 Underpinning these positions, it is therefore not only humanity in general who becomes the actor of the celebration, but the people of such and such a time, with their specific values, in the cycle of civilization in which we entered. So there is a fierce reaction against the "spiritualism" of past centuries. The awareness of humanity mastering the forces of nature through science, technologies, and economies, provokes in Christians, in their faith but also in their liturgy, a salutary shock, which is awakening in them the original realism of their mystery. The human being is not a spirit lodged in a body, it is a being where the body is consubstantially united with the spirit. Humanity is not placed within a universe whose determinations remain foreign to it; humanity is engaged in the construction of this world as its own, humanizing work. Humanity is not once and for all constituted by nature; by this very nature, as a work of intelligence, the human person is seized by the progress of history, finding there, personally and even more so collectively, fulfillment and happiness. How can the reference to their deity, which makes up the foundation of religion, and thus worship, not be renewed by this renewal of humanity, where they are, as human beings, actors in the liturgy and thereby continuators of the mystery? This is where a certain spiritualism, quickly turned into eternalism, is surprising, and sometimes shocking. We see it daily, in the liturgical reform underway, and in meeting the vigorous affirmation of the Council. "The church likewise, living in various conditions of history, has adopted the discoveries of various cultures to . . . express it [the message of Christ] better

in liturgical celebration and in the life of the varied community of the faithful." (*Gaudium et Spes*, 58)[2]

8 Whatever the problems, doctrinal and practical, for this redefinition of the liturgy, we must first go to the basis of this *aggiornamento*, in the very economy of Christianity: when God speaks to humanity, the Word is not shaped by its divine being, but by the human spirit with whom it enters into communication. "Per hominem more hominum loquitur" ([God] speaks to humanity according to nature of humanity), says St. Augustine.[3] Word of God, human word: obviously hearing first of all the texts and contexts of Scripture; where this Word is inscribed, but also the Tradition which is born within and by the lively interpretation of this Scripture; finally hear the liturgy, a mystery in action whose re-presentation emanates from Scripture, recapitulates Tradition, and expresses the aspirations, the distresses, and the hopes of contemporary humanity as well as those of previous generations.

9 Here we are at the beginning of the Christian economy, as it presents itself not only to the believer, but also already to the historian and to the phenomenologist of religions. When God, out of love, takes the initiative to propose participation in God's life to humanity, and already in the creative operation, God enters into the play of the laws of love, which want "the other" to condition my love; to achieve this communion with humanity, God becomes a human being. This means that this divine life in common is organized according to human structures: physical and mental, individual and collective, historical and prospective. Grace, says scholastic theology, is an "accident," that is to say, is implanted in a subject whose substance will be both the support and the rule of existence. Faith is expressed, constructed, communicated,

2. This sensitivity to the evolution of cultures is one of the points where the later works of the Council will have to refract onto the interpretation of the texts and the thought of the liturgical constitution, elaborated at the beginning of the Council, before the full effectiveness of its inspiration. Translators' note: our translation of *Gaudium et Spes* is taken from Norman P. Tanner, ed., *Decrees of the Ecumenical Councils: Volume 2 (Trent–Vatican II)* (London: Sheed and Ward, 1990), 1109.

3. Augustine, *City of God*, XVIII, 6, 2.

despite its fundamental irreducibility, according to the laws and behavior of the mind, in images, symbols, concepts and proposals, the fragility of which will not diminish the communion with the revealed Truth. God, says St. Thomas,[4] observes the law of knowledge according to which it is the knowing subject, and not the object in itself, who decides on the modes and methods of initiation. The metaphysical formulation of this principle only manifests the universal and radical application, in the faith of the believer, according to their historical existence as well as in individual being and collective existence. Today's humanity poses new questions to the Church, to the Church's liturgy as well as to catechesis and theology.

. . . In History

10 This questioning of humanity, hearer of the Word and actor, in this twentieth century, of the celebration, stems from the new awareness it has gained of its existence in history, i.e., of the dimension that its perfection accomplishes through its active participation in the construction of the world, in the development of society and in the collective advancement of peoples.

11 This very historicity implies that the human person defines themself *in* the world, not only as in a neutral place, which they occasionally inhabit, but as the domain of their co-creative power, and simultaneously as the resources of their humanization. So that this evolving cosmos in turn finds its meaning through human history.

12 Now the mystery of Christ, God who came into the world and into history, is, for the believer, the adequate response to humanity's double challenge. The celebration of the mystery today must manifest the ongoing recapitulation in Christ incarnate, until the end of time, of human history and of the cosmos that it engages. It is at this depth—in the faith and in the world that is coming—that the renewal of the liturgy is situated, well beyond the most necessary adaptations. It must be for the new consciousness of humanity, the cultic representation of the new creation. The *homo technicus* must be part of the *homo liturgicus*.

4. Thomas Aquinas, *Summa Theologiae*, IIa IIae, q. 1, a. 2.

13 It is here, at the juncture of nature and history, that the originality of Christian worship, the sacramental presence of the mystery of the God-Man, intervenes in the human person in liturgical action.

14 There are in fact two types of religion, and thus two different types of worship. There is the religion which emanates from the nature of humanity, as soon as it enters into contact with the divinity: humanity reveres, fears, invokes, desires the God who seems to them to command their destiny as God created their very being. Humanity's needs, aspirations, distresses, and hopes carry it towards this religion, through social contexts and psychological conditioning which, too often, deteriorate the representations which humanity made for itself. Despite its healthy spontaneities, the cult hardly escapes this deterioration. It tends to become a device to capture the favor of this formidable God (magic), to escape the adverse forces of nature (superstition) and to respect taboos. In any case, it is accomplished in a sacralization of things and people, leaving profane realities to their fate.

15 Of a completely different type is the religion which proceeds from faith, that is to say from listening to the Word of God. It is no longer humanity who ascends to divinity; it is God, a personal God, who, on God's own initiative, enters into conversation and communion with human beings, and, according to the law of this love, becomes a human being, as we have said, so that the deification is done by and in the humanization of God. We are then in history: this coming of God is an "event"; history is the homogeneous dimension of the operation, and no longer is that nature driven by its needs. Faith is the expressed recognition of this relationship. It inserts the personal history of the believer in a holy history, so that they become the collaborator of the creative drawing; but it leaves the human person in their worldly condition, even when sanctifying it, while religion introduces, already even in language, a break between the sacred and the profane. Christ invests the human being in all their existence, beyond all sacredness; he recapitulates all the values, and, collecting human history, thereby collects the cosmos which was its material. The incarnation brings the new creation to completion. The mystery continues in the time of history.

16 Worship, in this mystery, is obviously of a different order—in structure and in spirit—than that of "religion": it will be the memory and the re-presentation of the events of God, of the unique event of the incarnation, of the death and resurrection of the God-Man. No doubt faith will have to be embodied in the sacred, and naturalistic rites will be resumed to give a human surface to the expression of holy history, according to the logic of the humanization of the mystery. But, in its communion with the mystery, faith will be held in permanent transmutation of rites and gestures. Far from separating from the routine of profane life, it will realize, according to its object and in a total commitment, the presence in the world, both of the Christian personally and of the Community-Church. The sacraments will only have meaning and value through a conscious reference to a reality—*res sacramenti*—which is that of life itself in Christ, bringing together the universe to the glory of the Father and restoring all the values of the original creation.[5]

17 It will therefore be necessary to closely discern , at the very moment of their mutual involvement, the two sources of the Christian liturgy: that which makes it flow from the birth, death, and resurrection of Christ, a mystery in action today in the Body of Christ, and that which emanates in the rites and operations in use in any "natural" religion. It is clear that, when performing a ritual ensemble like mass, a sacred meal and a memory of the mystery, a rigorous discernment will be required in the renewal of symbols, acts, gestures, and words. The withering away of a certain sacredness, unimaginable and insensible in a technical mentality, will not compromise the permanent truth of the Eucharist. The sacred is archaic, hieratic, esoteric, while the mystery is in history, and, out of fidelity to itself, engaged in its evolutions.[6]

5. Translators' note: Chenu includes a note here directing his readers to the section headed "Liturgical Expression," albeit as though that section had the title "The Specifically Christian of Worship."

6. The word has been purged of its ambiguities in the wording of *Gaudium et Spes*, which uses it repeatedly, intentionally, despite the objections of some, precisely to define the articulation of the incarnation and the recapitulation in the one mystery of Christ.

The Human Condition

18 No more than one can describe the most spiritual actions of a human being, the ways they understand things as well as their loves by disregarding their body, one cannot determine and regulate the liturgical act by considering all the gestures, behaviors and symbolic games that make it up as simple and adventitious external expressions of a spiritual operation. Worship includes in its very substance the reality, burdensome and exciting, of the life of the body, with all its components. This corporeality, in all its forms and according to its own laws, is really the cause, and not only the condition, of the human and sacred intensity of the liturgical act. This is not only because the whole human being is composed of body and soul, and therefore, for a total homage to God, the body too must be committed to it, but also because the act itself includes the body to be *true* in humanity: blessing, raising hands, taking bread, washing, kneeling, standing, etc. This is the nature of the liturgical gesture: more than a role to play in "giving substance" to the sacred which is otherwise conceived, it is, at various levels, the sacred in action. More than "form," "matter" is, so to speak, the living flesh of the sacraments.[7]

19 The gesture, without doubt, is not raw material, in a mechanical execution; it is meaning, that is to say spiritual density engaged and represented in matter, which exceeds itself in this seductive exaltation. Like a kiss. Like a communal meal, so loaded with human implications, even when everyday banality renders them unconscious, where the material utility of nutrition obviously takes precedence over communal indulgence. But, in any case, we observe the expression and the exercise of the human condition in a psychological and ontological behavior subject to all the variants of temperaments, mentalities, geographical and cultural backgrounds (hence the variety and evolution of the liturgies), owing to the fact that, in humanity, the spirit is, as the philosophers say, the "form" of an organized body. The eminent dignity of matter,

7. It is obvious to refer here to the text of St. Thomas on fundamental anthropology: *Summa Theologiae,* IIIa, q. 60, a. 4, corp. and ad I.

not only in its density of being, but in its capacity for symbolic representation, is truly the subject of our acts of worship.

20 From this will flow not only a set of practical requirements for the proper execution of gestures with the elocution that accompanies them, but also a subtle sensitivity to the symbolic implications of their functional articulation: taking bread and eating it is not done properly without observing, down to the details, certain manners and customs; they must not be obscured by the premature play of a spiritualization which evacuates the heaviness of matter and its coarse symbolisms. A certain way of receiving the Eucharistic bread, and already of making it a "host," dissolves the realism of the meal where one eats, at the same time as it reflects a bad theology of transubstantiation.[8] Dehumanizing the sacraments, large or small, is certainly not respecting their nature. A whole liturgical psychology of the gesture, of the figurative gesture of the mystery, is developed from this philosophy of the body.[9] The fate of the liturgy depends on it.

21 If the Christian, if the Church as a community of Christians, must hold this position in worship, for the coherence, if not for the orthodoxy, of their faith, and therefore to consent to a certain anthropology,[10] neither the faith nor the Church has to provide a systematic interpretation of this conception of humanity. It is up to the theologian to do this, or even to the Christian who seeks to

8. Long ago, in the first days of the liturgical renewal, Father Doncœur published with his customary intrepidity, a brilliant article on the human realism of baptism by immersion, compared with the tiny drop of water which obviously cannot retain the symbol. The rubricists put a curse on him. Translators' note: Chenu seems to be referring to Paul Doncœur, "La catéchèse du baptême," *La Maison-Dieu* 16 (1948): 48–59.

9. Not having to indicate here the works on the philosophy of the body or on the function of the gesture (and of the hand) in general, let us refer to our very subject, in doctrine and in practice, to André Laurentin, *La liturgie en chantier. Les gestes du célébrant*, Paroisse et liturgie 68 (Saint-André: Biblica, 1965).

10. Anthropology: we take the word here in its general sense, indeed vigorous, of conception of humanity. All philosophy includes an anthropology. In the contemporary diversification of philosophical disciplines and because of their opposing options, the word has become particularized alongside or opposite a philosophy of history, a philosophy of nature.

explain the content of their faith—in the case of the sacramentality of the mystery—by resorting to a philosophy of the human, to a sociology of worship, to a psychology of the sacred, to a theology of history. A council does not have to engage in such research, but simply to bear witness to the faith. However, this "scholastic" theology of the sacrament and the liturgy should not be depreciated, nor even neglected, as it is not "pastoral." The worst would then be to do theology—and philosophy—without knowing it.

22 It is therefore important to identify and explain the philosophies of the human being which may be at work in liturgical life, and which are able to explain the rites, gestures, and symbols articulated in the sacramental ensembles. St. Thomas, whom we have just quoted, founds the necessity of the sacraments on the principle of Aristotelian noetics according to which the sensible is the indispensable way of access to the intelligible, in a being where the spirit is the "form" of the body. If, on the contrary, we hold a dualist philosophy of matter and spirit, the interpretation of the liturgy and its signs will be modified, in the appreciation of their mechanism and their value. Thus, we might observe with good reason that the era of Cartesian spirituality and its by-products in the nineteenth century is contemporaneous with the worst decadence of liturgical understanding in modern times. Think about the reforms undertaken by the Enlightenment and the "sacristan king" Joseph II.[11]

23 Without dwelling on this impact of philosophies of the human condition on the theological elaboration of the cultic enterprise, let us note nevertheless, in the main axis of the relations between the sensible and the intelligible, and therefore of the decisive connection between rite and mystery, the profound difference between the two mentalities which permeated Christian behavior in the West. According to the line of Aristotelianism, the coherence between the sensible gesture and the mysterious reality is, in its radical interiority, the solid and permanent natural ground of a religious spirituality. We will not then be inclined to deviate from a realistic interpretation of gestures, images, or sacralizations. On

11. Translators' note: Chenu appears to be referring to Joseph II, who as the Habsburg Emperor reigned 1765–1790.

the other hand, in a Platonic mentality, according to which matter is only a heavy conditioning of the spirit, one risks giving way to a certain occasionalism, where the rite will only be a provocation to spiritual transfers. But also, in this philosophy of participation where the degrees of being are linked to each other by analogical resemblances, symbolism will be the normal means of passing from the one to the other, and will become the basic operation of representation, mental or gestural, of the mystery, in rites of initiation and illumination. In this mystical pedagogy, the sensible and the imaginary will have a power that noetic materialism and Aristotle's conceptual abstraction could not confer. Dionysius is the master here. We know what role he played among Christian theologians, both in the interpretation of rites and in the philosophy of religion. St. Thomas, who had initially believed him to be an Aristotelian, considered him, not without some concordance with the Philosopher, as an "authority" on which to base his theology of the sacraments. So, from the start, he quoted him. "Et inde est quod ad sacramenta requiruntur res sensibiles, *ut etiam Dionysius probat*" (And it is because of this that sensible realities are needed for the sacraments. This is also demonstrated by Dionysius).[12] In fact, we find in Dionysius a very keen sense of the function and the original laws of the symbol, even if it means recognizing in his analyses the limits of his mystagogical neoplatonism.

24 One question cannot but be asked here, in this philosophical approach of the theologian: Why not have recourse, first of all, to biblical anthropology? Is it not this which, like Scripture itself, must permeate the human expression of the liturgy, words and gestures, matter and form? It is quite true that the original homogeneity of Scripture and liturgy provides a presumption in favor of the psychological categories of the *homo biblicus*. It goes without saying, moreover, that the system of representations and cultic actions of the Old Covenant and of the early Christian community served as a model, directly or indirectly, sometimes as a legal rule, for the Church's liturgy, due to its constant reading of Scripture.

12. Thomas Aquinas, *Summa Theologiae*, IIIa, q. 60, a. 4. Translators' note: the published French text includes the minor typographical error in quoting Thomas's Latin here as "res sensibilis."

For example, the general pattern of the revelation of the mystery in a story, including the facts and gestures of the old memory and the gestures of the new one, will enter into the liturgical fabric. Similarly, the theory of four senses of Scripture, not only in exegesis but in liturgy. However, the typically Semitic categories of biblical anthropology do not impose themselves in the operations or in the definition of the Christian *homo liturgicus*. Disqualifying a dualistic analysis of the human being, we do not consider as a given of faith the tripartite conception of St. Paul, who discerned in the human condition *sarx*, *psyche*, and *nous*; equally his theology of *pneuma* does not include a philosophy of *spiritus*, even though these categories provide valuable resources for the understanding of humanity gripped by the mystery. There as elsewhere, we are at this mobile frontier where faith, in its transcendence, enters into the free play of human intelligence and its autonomous vision of the world. We will have different "theologies," let us say here: different liturgical anthropologies, even if it means measuring their capacity to account for the existence and structures of acts of worship. Thus, a certain analysis of the games of the image in the dynamic of reason (I am thinking of the suggestive categories of *ratio inferior* and *ratio superior* in medieval philosophy) has what it takes to account excellently for the articulation of images and symbols in the figurative expression of the mystery. On the other hand, as we say, Cartesian dualism does not seem to be able to ground the perfect interference of matter and spirit, worship and contemplation, in the very unified liturgical act of the believer.

An essential feature of the human condition, closely linked moreover to corporeality, must finally be noted: the human person can only be a human person *in* the world. "Being-in-the-world" is more than an attribute, it is, in the most technical sense of the word, a condition of being human. We know what importance contemporary philosophies, of whatever persuasion, attach to this cosmic dimension. We would go so far as to say that the human person in an act of worship perfectly illustrates this position, all the more so since, in this act, they are in a state of reference to the divinity outside the world. That is, then, a categorical refusal of anthropologies, Christian or not, which distinguish in the human soul two zones, almost two faculties, one turned towards God and the Spirit, the other turned towards the earthly realities recorded by the so-called sensitive faculties. The liturgist will not fail to meditate on this problem and this position when they seek to understand the *caelestia-terrestria* dialectic, so frequent in their vocabulary. They will gladly do so, moreover, for they feel healthy when the whole cosmos, in space and time, one might say, enters into their sacred perceptions and into their mysterious vision.

26 Far from being distressed by it, the liturgist—better still, every Christian in the liturgical act—revels in this tension, fearing above all that the sacralization, or even the consecration, that they bring to bear on things will set them so far apart that they lose their terrestrial and human density. The liturgical elements retain the native and fresh authenticity that they had in the universe from which they are drawn. We must, however, detach them from their technical use, from the wear and tear of our ordinary lives, which may have damaged their meaning: human reality is transfigured, and becomes theophany. Hence this dialectic: things are set apart from human use by their sacred reference, but the original human experience and meaning must remain perceptible, under pain of an "alienation" which distorts the sacred itself.[13] Religions have hardly escaped this failure.

27 Let us go to the principle of this demanding operation. It is in the nature of humanity, and therefore of human religious nature, not only to look at the world, but to be in it, not only to develop one's energies in it, but to be a micro-cosmos to flow in the physical and biological rhythms of the world, in the cycles of time, of seasons, and of fertility, to make these rhythms one's own as so many instances of sacralization. The historian of religions documents for us abundantly the myths and rituals of this meaning of creation. The Christian theologian denounces the abusive sacralizations, sources of magic and superstition, even under the Christian system; but they do not reject, in their liturgy, the references to times and seasons, as long as they are and remain, in faith, the implications of the mystery of Christ, recapitulator of

13. Cf. Laurentin, *La liturgie en chantier*, 117ff., which illustrates this principle with numerous practical cases.

history, and, in the human being, of all creation (cf. Rom 8:18-25). Reading the Liturgical Constitution in the light of the cosmic Christology of the Constitution *Gaudium et Spes,* one will bring out an unexpected intensity: the enterprise of the construction of the world ends in the paschal mystery (GS 38).

Expressions and Representations

28 If such is the human condition, all the registers of human activities will be controlled and penetrated by this structure, both in the intellectual life and in the affective life. See the philosophers. Among all these registers, the most striking, and certainly not the least human, will perhaps be that of the representations and knowledge obtained by means of signification, in which affectivity and intelligibility are combined: an immense and varied domain, with its specific characteristics, in which, without further ado, we situate all the liturgical operations. The liturgy is indeed based on signs, "sacraments," in the original sense of the word. We have seen its anthropological underpinnings above; let us now briefly observe its various modalities, from the perspective of the mystery to be represented.

29 First reflection: *signification* is of a different order than *explanation.* The two paths will overlap, but they are psychologically heterogeneous, in their processes and in their resources. Explanation is a search for causes, internal or external, which will account for the nature and properties of a thing or an action. It is expressed in concepts and develops in science, whose certainties, to varying degrees, impose themselves on the capacity for understanding. Signification does not proceed by analysis, nor does it seek proofs; it develops in the relationship between two realities, one of which, whatever its natural content, is supposed to represent another, situated in a different order of things. The ontological or psychological unevenness is the very basis of the accomplished mental transfer. Taking the hand is a physical act, which the doctor can do to exercise his profession; but it becomes a "gesture," if by it I mean my friendship, or my protection, or my impatience. So standing up, sitting down, joining hands, having a meal. While the explanation

tends to a precise and unique determination, in a pure objectivity, the signification proliferates in multiple senses, according to the circumstances, the persons, the intentions, the relations involved; and this subjective versatility can manifest itself in disparate arrangements of references, as opposed to conceptual definitions. Fire is the symbol of love, anger, punishment, exaltation; water purifies, submerges, quenches thirst; the lamb evokes, unlike the sheep, multiple images and feelings. Fantasy, harmful to science, provides here an admirable fruitfulness, and its creations are endlessly repeated. Not to mention the specific register of signs uttered in language and song, social life is daily filled with signs, the multiplication of which is commensurate with relationships and gatherings.

30 The liturgy is of the order of signification. *Sacramenta sunt in genere signi*, say the theologians;[14] sacraments as such, but also any "ceremony." The obviousness of this definition does not, however, block the problem of the "explanation" called for by the understanding of these signs: origin, structure, scope, value, aesthetics. Let us return to the philosophers who today study with perspicacity the ways and means of signification. Let us simply observe that we are at the principle of the originality of the liturgical act: it cannot be resolved into an explanation, nor into knowledge, nor into a unilinear development; it depends on an "initiation," and, as much as possible, remains under its influence. The scientist will not be complacent about it; the "catechisms" will hardly predispose to it; rubricists will fear the fantasy of its symbols. This is now a classic and far-reaching thesis, which we link here to its anthropological foundation.

31 Second reflection. Contrary to explanation, to the search for causes, to a definition set out in concepts, meaning makes good use of images. It is even the place where it is most fruitful, because abstract signs, such as words, numbers, and lines, still harbor primitive imaginations. The human, certainly, is reason; to deviate from reason, or even to mistrust it, is to run the risk of becoming dehumanized. But reason is precisely defined as an intelligence

14. Translators' note: that is, "sacraments are in the category of signs." See, for example, Thomas Aquinas, *Summa Theologiae*, IIIa, q. 60, a. 1, co.

immersed in the sensible, from which it must, by repeated abstractions, draw its ideas. Signs, in their raw state, are infra-rational; they feed on the spontaneity of our multiple instincts, even in their biological consonance. To rationalize them is to devitalize them in their very source, even if it means that, one day, they will take their revenge, as we see today in the reactions against rationalizations of any caliber. An old and ever-new quarrel. Theologians are no exception, nor are liturgists. Images have their laws, the interplay of which is not without order, nor, of course, without beauty. If the liturgy is a set of signs of the relationship with the divinity—with God incarnate, for the Christian—we can foresee the power, heady and ambiguous, of the representations and figures, gestures included: true theophanies, said the ancients.[15] The more they are rooted in human soil, flesh and spirit, the more likely they are to be not only effective, but true. How to achieve such a "celebration"?

32 Let us give full meaning here—this is our third reflection—to the term which, in this proliferation of images, will designate their specific point: in this domain of the imaginary, *the symbol* is the most decisive representation of the sacred, of the Christian mystery. Sign, symbol: although theologians pass from one word to the other, and although the Latins, following Augustine, have almost exclusively used the first, we can distinguish them even in their resemblance. On this, the development of literary genres and aesthetic forms provides copious material for analysis. Let us note this single observation: the symbol, spoken or acted, proceeds from a metaphor, that is to say from a transfer by which the spirit, imagination, and intelligence, passes, by a kind of provocation, from one reality to another, thanks to their analogy. "The Word of God *is* a seed . . ." and not: "The Word of God is *like* a seed . . . ," which would fall back to a comparison, which, for its part, is of the order of explanation, no longer of signification. The fire that devours me, says the lover; and not: My love is like a fire. Literary trick? Yes, but expressing through metaphor the leap of spirit and heart. Hence the realism of the symbol, particularly of the symbolic gesture, to which no explanation can be adequate, even if it

15. Reproduced by Laurentin, *La liturgie en chantier*, 117, 119, *passim*.

becomes necessary. Ultimately, if a symbol requires an explanation, it has failed. It is indeed according to the human condition that the mystery finds a homogeneous expression in the symbol.

33 Before we look at the essential articulation of the liturgical act, let us be clear about the all-too-frequent confusion between symbol and allegory, even if a certain allegorization normally reinforces its meaning. This discernment is all the more urgent given that, for centuries, liturgical symbolism has yielded to this drift, in conditions that have corrupted its very nature. History teaches us good lessons. While the symbol plays according to the figuration of its basic image, the allegory devotes itself to the analysis of the material elements of this image, to find a meaning for each one. Bread is the symbol of the meal; but I can analyze its color, shape, chemical composition, manufacture, and give a particular meaning to each of these properties. The paschal candle is no longer the figure of the Christ-light in his resurrection; it is composed of the wax, which is his body, of the wick, which is his soul, of the flame, which is his divinity. Such an allegory transforms the first sensitive perception and its impulsive vigor into a refined intellectual operation. Thus we were able, in the past, to explain the sacrifice of the mass by finding there one by one the episodes of the passion, thanks to this alchemy of abstractions. There is no worse fouling of the liturgical mystery than this irrelevant intellectualization.

Liturgical Expression

Mystery, Symbol, Rite

34 Alas, it is not paradoxical to speak of "practitioners" who are not (or barely) "believers," and of "believers" who are not "practitioners." In truth, it is not easy to articulate, if one has clearly distinguished them, religion and faith, religion emanating from nature, faith being communion with the mystery of God in history. How, then, will the unity of the liturgical act be constituted?

35 Because the distortion of rite and mystery is not merely the unfortunate effect of the faithful's lukewarmness, numbed to sacred practices. Considering them in their initial tenor, they develop along different trajectories, to the point that religion (the cult),

with its sacralizations, runs the risk of deadening the mystery, and faith (the mystery) of being no more than the object of a vague aspiration, without real commitment or presence in the world.

36 It is in the symbol, gestural or verbal, that, according to the human condition, rite and mystery are tied. This is why we have set ourselves the task of measuring its originality, in which its homogeneity with mystery becomes perfectly clear. The symbolic value, we said, is taken from the distance between the thing-sign and the reality-mystery, from the hiatus experienced between the two, and which imposes like a leap from the visible material thing to a certain deep density and will provoke the transfer to the hidden reality. An exhilarating rise, charged with affectivity, which can only be achieved in and through "initiation," not through indoctrination (which is, for the most part, of the type of science). Poetic power, to the extent that a liturgy that is not born poetically is a failure. Power of exaltation, too, which bursts forth in joy, and is, as it were, released in celebration. The symbol is not an accessory ornament of the mystery, nor a provisional pedagogy; it is the coessential resource of its communication. Such is the depth of the psychological and ontological insertion of the ritual symbol into the mystery.

37 Ritual symbol, we say, because the symbol cannot stand in its effervescence; it is fixed in rites, which provide it with both consistency in the person and communicability in the assembly. "Religion" then becomes the place of incarnation of faith; even if it means conditioning it, geographically, sociologically, culturally, conceptually. But faith draws on these ritual devices to transcend them in a "Christian" transmutation. It will carry out a "spiritual worship," which is certainly not a disincarnation, nor a desacramentalization, but rather communion in the mystery of Christ, thus visibly witnessed by the people of God, a communion nourished by effective representations, in a presence in the world.

38 If the mystery is and remains thus present, it is because the symbol procures its expression in the continuity of time. It is not an artificial, "spiritual" prolongation by a fervent imagination: time effectively enters the mystery's structure, and ritual symbolic action is its means. The sacrament is the intermediary between mystery and history; the symbolism is enfleshed in the mystery as

the mystery is in time. The rite constructs this effective symbolism in coordinated actions. Such is the coherence of the symbol and of the presence, of the mysterious presence. The mystery, the mystery of the death and resurrection of Christ, needs the symbol to be present. Whence the law of the spiritual density of the rite: it is entirely in the vigor of the symbol.

39 But also the symbol, to fulfill its function, must be spontaneously, and not only intellectually, the expression of the human in the world and in time. If it is an archaeological reconstruction, or a mental escape, it disarticulates the whole operation, and the cult falls back to its "ritual" gravity. The adaptation of liturgical reforms to the traditions of different peoples, in space and time (cf. SC 37) finds its foundation and its requirements here.

40 Final reflection. This primacy of the symbol, with all the contexts of the imaginary, should not cause subsequent conceptualization to be depreciated. Just as faith does not fear, but, in order to be adult, calls for an intelligibility which organizes itself into knowledge, so liturgical initiation maintains in its maturity a permanent instruction and catechesis. Such is the itinerary of signification, religious or not, according to the human condition. The *mythos* is expressed and affirmed in *logos*. The mystery is constructed in "reasons." Thus, the messianic "myth," the primary fabric of the Judaeo-Christian economy, needs mental as well as liturgical representations. A certain intellectuality of the symbol is necessary; it is up to the realism of the liturgical *act* to guarantee it against idealism and its abstractions.

Social Humanity

41 If humanity is, by nature, in the world and in history, humanity is, by nature, in society. The person only exists and develops within communities. These axioms are one and the same.

42 Let us therefore continue our enterprise, in this anthropology of cult. Worship, religion, the mystery of the God-*Man* of history, will grasp humanity in its social nature. The human face of the liturgy will be an assembly. It is in an assembly that the mystery is accomplished. The Church is a people, not an aggregate of individual salvations. The absolute personalism of faith and love will

no more be defeated by this collectivism than the dignity of the person will be threatened by socialization, wherever it is true.[16]

43 In this very collection, Fr. Congar provides the record of the Tradition showing that it is the *ecclesia* which is the subject of liturgical acts, without detriment to the "powers," then shows on what Christological foundations the essential law of the active participation of the faithful in the assembly is established. *Quod omnes tangit ab omnibus tractari et approbari debet.* (What affects all must be dealt with and approved by all.)[17]

44 We need only repeat this principle and its foundations here to underline its topicality. In other words: according to the law of the mystery of Christ, which is underway in his Body today, all the values of humanity are assumed in this permanent recapitulation, as and when they emerge, thanks to symbolic representations. At all times, human beings have lived in society; and from its first days, the Christian liturgy was celebrated in community. But today this social dimension of humanity has assumed massive proportions; "socialization" is the common denominator of the transformations of the world, not only in technical progress, but also in the culture of the spirit. The intensity and rapidity of the phenomenon make it dramatic, and its excesses provoke strong reactions, including in the "inner life" of Christians. We cannot, however, be unfaithful to the logic of our position: this communal humanization gives the liturgy an unprecedented chance in relation to the era of individualistic spirituality from which we are moving away. After the Constitution *Gaudium et Spes*, which is built on the analysis of the transformations of the world into an

16. Cf. Constitution *Gaudium et Spes* 32: the human community, Christ entering into this solidarity.

17. Translators' note: Chenu is here referring to one of Yves Congar's contributions to the volume in which his essay was originally published; see Yves M.-J. Congar, "L''Ecclesia' ou communauté chrétienne sujet integral de l'action liturgique," in *La liturgie après Vatican II: Bilans, études, prospective*, ed. Jean-Pierre Jossua and Yves Congar (Paris: Cerf, 1967), 241–88. In English translation, see Yves Congar, "The *Ecclesia* or Christian Community as a Whole Celebrates the Liturgy," in *At the Heart of Christian Worship: Liturgical Essays of Yves Congar*, ed. Paul Philibert (Collegeville, MN: Liturgical Press, 2010), 15–68.

act of questioning the Church, we can give even more vigor, and, for its application, more precision, to the liturgical Constitution, which sees in the *ecclesia* the integral subject of liturgical action.

In the truth of the mystery and the reality of history, therefore, anthropological analysis renders more vivid and more lucid, the demands of the renewal of the liturgy.

For a Sacramental Anthropology (1974)[1]

Para no.

1 Now that we have come to grips with the proper level of Christian mystery, its interior consistency, its specific values, I am going to introduce rationality into the mix, which is a devaluation. As I was listening to you, and as I became more and more involved in the mystery, the rational analysis I am about to propose seemed rather miserable. And yet this intelligibility, however heterogeneous it may be at first glance, finds its logic deep in the understanding of mystery. This is really the theologian's task: to speak humanly about divine values. At this lower level, I am going to propose four reflections, with reference to St. Thomas who, in this rationality, has a very original approach, irreducible to all the

1. This text is the "reportage," as they used to say in the Middle Ages, of an interview in which we had deliberately given in to suggestions, which were certainly well founded, but lacked appropriate analyses and references. By publishing it, we have resisted the temptation to rewrite it to give it better consistency, or literary quality. We would like to agree to these limits. The subtitles are from the editorial staff of the journal.

For further reflection, the reader may refer to some of our previous contributions which have addressed these questions.

Translators' note: the original note lists the other essays that we have included in this volume. We are not aware of any verbatim publication of the interview that would clarify the context of the "reportage." This essay was republished unedited by *La Maison-Dieu* in 2020 in their special 300th edition, with an introduction by Monique Brulin, "Marie-Dominique Chenu 'Pour une anthropologie sacramentelle' (LMD 119, 1974, 85–100)," *La Maison-Dieu* 300 (2020): 171–89.

theologians of his time, and who was condemned precisely over his anthropology.

The Raison d'être of Sacramentality

2 According to St. Thomas, the sacramental order, not only the seven sacraments but sacramentality as a whole, finds its raison d'être or—to take the language and the pedagogical categories of that time—its necessity as well as its structure in this absolute principle: "God provides for every reality according to its mode of being,"[2] be it its nature, of its very being, whether it concerns its situation, its condition, its behaviors. These are naturally linked, since being is found to be expressed in behaviors.

3 Almost all theologians say this, but St. Thomas says it with great rigor, which often was weakened in ordinary Thomism. According to him, it is a general law of God's economy, of God's plan, whether in creation or in the incarnation, a law that radically commands the totality of the divine enterprise: when God does something that emanates a being, God does so not according to God's condition to that being, as creator and redeemer, but according to the condition of the being he has just created. There is a kind of extroversion here: God will only be present through the very reality that God has created and God will confer his life through perceptible realities, through matter. It is necessary to give depth to this word "matter," as it is much more interesting than the pair matter and form, which introduced a low-class Aristotelianism into sacramental theology and, alas, into the conciliar texts. The created being will have to resort to matter and its inclination, by the very fact, will always tend towards matter. Secondly, matter must serve to divert the human being from their inclination to superstition, to magic, as if we were giving matter the mechanical power to dominate even the divine life. Here we see the salubrity of St. Thomas's message, even on a purely human level: it is salubrious that there are sacraments, for the very authenticity of the

2. Translators' note: Chenu is referring to texts such as Thomas Aquinas, *Summa Theologiae*, IIIa, q. 61, a. 1, resp.

manipulation of matter, and to free humanity from superstition, so widespread, even among Christians.

4 It is only thirdly that the sacraments are justified as remedies. Here we leave the order of natures and the emanation of being to move on to a reflection from Augustinianism. Of all the theologians of his time, St. Thomas is the only one not to give it priority.

5 Here we have an anthropology in the global sense of the term, a science of humanity, giving its intensity to the word "human." The term anthropology is fairly new for theology, but it is very much appropriate. Sacramental anthropology: this term takes on its full depth, not as an illustration of a previously known sacramental reality, but as a co-essential aspect of the sacrament. We can only engage the sacrament in consubstantiality with the human. The two words "anthropology" and "sacramental" are inseparable from each other not only in terms of methods—that would already be valuable—but constitutively. Both in its radical being and in all its functions and sensitivities, sacramentality refers to being human. The regulation of the sacrament and the sacramental life, in the distribution, exercise, functioning and ritualizations, is not to be sought in God but in humanity. And this is also true for the Word of God, as St. Augustine admirably said: "When God speaks to humans, he speaks in the manner of humans."[3] One could draw a parallel between the sacramental anthropology of St. Thomas and the early efforts of the Carolingian Renaissance to apply the laws of grammar to the understanding of the Word of God.

6 It follows that the humanities are not simply an illustration or a rational instrument annexed to sacramental theology: it is fully right that the human sciences are included in it as an essential component of reflection—a component not only of theological deduction at the end, but from the start. The more theology is theology, the more the humanities will have a right to intervene in it, and the more I advance in theological perspicacity the more my human sciences will be autonomous, I was going to say secularized in this autonomy. This is enough to allay the fears of some of my confrere-sociologists who fear that theologians will reclaim, in

3. Translators' note: cf. Augustine, *City of God*, XVIII, 6, 2.

the pejorative sense of the word, the humanities and their results, by manipulating them: they have good reasons to fear because theologians have often done this, but by rights they should not. The more theology is theology, the more the humanities will be human, profane; the more God is God, the more the human being is human. If I have a God who shrivels humanity a little to bring us into the divine economy, this is a false God; and if my theology manipulates the humanities to order them, it is bad theology.

7 This extends widely and applies to the whole Christian economy and at the same time for everything. The whole Christian economy and the whole human condition are controlled by this. Everything in human existence passes through the senses, and I have nothing in my mind that has not passed through matter. You know the famous axiom of philosophers about the "tabula rasa": when I want to know something, I will look for it outside. We are the opposite of interiorism: everything I receive, including God, comes from outside. In being, in action, in epistemology: the whole epistemology is built on it, against practically all idealism. And it permeates the mental fabric of St. Thomas and his every reaction.

Determination and Establishment of the Sevenfold Sacramental Order

8 The great operation that took place in the West, in the twelfth and thirteenth centuries, in the sacramental field, was the determination of the sevenfold order of the sacraments, declared a dogma in 1215 at the Fourth Lateran Council. It was a magnificent operation, but an unfortunate one, too, in that the emergence of the seven sacraments devalued the rest of sacramentality. The elaboration of a *De sacramentis in genere* has been beneficial, but I think that, conversely, we should start from *De sacramentis in particulari* and only at the end start a general sacramentality. We did the opposite. In a beneficial way, moreover, we have also designed the whole of sacramentality, identified strategic points, obtained a global view of the sacramental economy, and at the same time given each sacrament its own consistency, its situation, and therefore its value.

9 On this, rationality seeps in: Why are there seven sacraments? All the theologians have said: it is because there are seven instances of sin that we need seven remedies: I am concupiscent, I am angry, proud, and each time I have a remedy for it. It is therefore a medicinal conception whereby the sacraments, according to the image of that time, are a pharmacopoeia containing all the remedies that Christ has given us. This is a critical issue, I would say, not stemming from Augustine, but from Augustinianism. According to a naturalistic principle, St. Thomas starts from episodes of vital growth in the individual and in collective humanity. Where the person humanizes themself, there needs to be a rite, from birth, which is the first act, until death. At each pivot of humanization there is a sacrament, which is there to deify.[4]

10 Since there are seven sacraments, St. Thomas found seven occasions, from baptism, which takes people at birth, until death, where the sick are anointed. Between the two, the other sacraments are arranged: first of all the Eucharist which is daily food, and which has a completely different aspect from baptism, which is given only once. In this way he constructs the originality of each sacrament. Two of these sacraments concern collective humanity; indeed, St. Thomas is very attentive to the social nature of humanity. A sacrament is to be situated in the very first and radical sociability, that of the couple sexualized for fertility: the sacrament of marriage. Another sacrament is constituted at the service of the people of God within humanity: the sacrament of Orders, through which the Word of God is transmitted. In our analysis of the anthropological dimension of the sacraments this is a great resource. Not that St. Thomas has foreseen everything, but because he offers us here a principle founding a theological radicalism beyond an already ambitious kind of phenomenology.

The Old Law and Its Theology of Worship

11 To answer our question, I took the patience—and one needs a lot—to closely reread the treatise on the Old Law, in the *Summa*

4. Cf. Thomas Aquinas, *Summa Theologiae*, IIIa, q. 65, a. 1.

Theologiae. The Old Law occupies a very large textual surface in St. Thomas, which is quite disconcerting. While in most of his articles, even on grace, there is one column or one and a half columns, there are five for each of the articles which analyze the Old Law. The Thomists never read all this, nor did they read the cosmogony in his treatise on Creation, or the life of Christ in the treatise on the incarnation. They de-biblicized the *Summa Theologiae* and, reducing it to its speculative parts, they evacuated its historical realism.

12 Let us take a few examples. St. Thomas introduces critical categories to find the rationality of all the elements of the Old Law, in particular of Deuteronomy, and of classifications which I am reporting for the sake of scholarship. He distinguishes between the *moralia*, the *iudicialia* and the *ceremonialia*. The *moralia* concern human conduct, morality in the broadest sense of the word, including the relationship with God. The *iudicialia* concern socio-political organization, and the *ceremonialia*, what pertains to the cult. On the basis of a critical analysis of the Old Law, St. Thomas establishes a theology of worship, which is of interest both as an operation in itself and because the Christian liturgy has inherited from it. The reflections of the Middle Ages on worship and the sacraments are saturated with references to the Old Testament, as is also the case for the reflections on the Church as theocracy, because the biblical theocracy was taken as a model of the Church, and was taken very seriously. Here we take the cultic theology of the ancient ceremonies to feed the sacramental analysis, even where it means denouncing the threat of deviation, or even more allegorizing. Such an operation devalues the investigation of the Old Testament by intellectualizing it, and in medieval theology the permanent allegorization is a perversion of its symbolic meaning, because the allegory plays by intellectualizing the symbol, which by itself should not be intellectualized, but stand in its own imaginary.

13 Reading the treatise, which is rather tedious, allows us to see what St. Thomas makes come from either nature or history, in other words from a messianic perspective: for example, in the analysis of the pure and the impure. This remains a sketch compared to the phenomenology of our contemporaries, but it is still very

effective. The critical axis is to uncover motivation and meaning. St. Thomas tells us what the raison d'être is, looking not for "causal" reasons, but for meaning-reasons. Spontaneously he resorts to signification—the raison d'être is signification—and analyzes the play of symbols, observing in particular the distance and discontinuity between the signifier and the signified, provoking a kind of jolt in which the symbol plays (this is the reason for the hidden element in this whole operation). Secondly, he analyzes the rite, triggered by this symbolic game: the link is very close between the two. In the ceremonial he analyzes the gestures more than the words, and he distinguishes the ritualized symbol, the essential gesture, from what he calls the "solemnity." He also appeals to another notion, that of the sacred, which is the property of being, of action and of things put in relation to divinity. The subject of the sacred is the body, and the reference to divinity happens through the mediation of the body.

14 By resorting to the empirical categories of time he draws a cultic geography of the various *ceremonialia*: first the sacrifices, then what he calls the *sacramenta*, then the *sacra* and the *observantiae*. In these theological categories, for example in the distinction between *sacramenta* and *sacra*, we find many useful things, sometimes arbitrary, but full of meaning. In the sacred, consideration is given not to this reference to God, which would seem to be decisive, but to the human condition. This is at play from one end to the other in this fabric, including references to collective life, for example to nomadism, which modifies the sacramental economy, or to the link between war and peace; to which are added, in their relationship to the human condition, the rhythms of nature, harvesting, springtime, sowing. Does the Old Testament recognize the duality introduced by the reference to nature? Our modern biblical scholars, G. von Rad, for example, think so.[5] St. Thomas has spotted this as a theologian, and it is important for the anatomy of the sacrament, but he risks devaluing these natural elements for the sake of the economy, for fear of superstitions—a

5. Translators' note: Chenu appears to be thinking of discussions such as those of Gerhard von Rad, *Old Testament Theology* (London: SCM, 1975), 232–34.

fear that the Old Testament itself already had—and it devalues pagan rites, whereas we tend to give them value today. In other words, the theology of St. Thomas is in every way a theology of established Christianity, including in his sacramental theology, and this is one of its limits. Many of our contemporary reflections would fit here. In any case, his method could be applied not only to the Old Testament, but also to the New, where he studies the ritualization of each sacrament.

Co-naturality of the Sensible in the Sacramental Economy

15 Let us resume the principle, laid down at the beginning, of the radical co-naturality of the sensible in the sacramental economy, namely that matter—what is called, in the sacramental language of the thirteenth century, *res sensibilis*—is the first component of the sacrament, long before the analysis of matter and form is introduced. At this point I will consciously give in to a philosophical "drift" that takes me completely away from the internal elaboration of faith such as Fr. Jourjon[6] did for Christian doctors, and rationalize to the extreme, instead of an internal elaboration of the faith, its domain, its knowledge. But, at the same time, I claim this operation as legitimate in theology, in intelligibility. One tried to exclude it from the texts of the Council: it is a chimera! When there is a philosophy without knowledge, it is likely to be bad.

First Component of the Sacrament

16 If matter, in every sense of the word, *res sensibilis,* and, for us, the human body, is the first essential component of the sacrament, an intelligibility different from matter will influence the understanding of the sacrament. If the sacrament is first of all matter, the way I conceive of matter will modify my understanding of the sacrament: either matter in itself, or matter in the cosmos, or of the matter in the human being, the body. And, depending on the

6. Translators' note: This is probably a reference to Maurice Jourjon, sometime Dean of the Faculty of Theology at Lyon and member of the ecumenical Groupe des Dombes.

ontological and psychological density that I will give to matter, I will have different sacramental theologies, not only in this psychological play, but in its inner intelligibility. If, for example, I am a dualist, in the most general sense of the word—it does not matter whether in the manner of the Platonists or that of Descartes—i.e., if I believe that the universe is composed of two things, with a border that is actually impenetrable even if there is a permanent interaction, I will have a completely different conception of the sacrament. Or, if I have an idealistic philosophy, or even, more generally, a spiritualist philosophy, I will look at matter differently, and therefore likewise at the sacraments. This is how St. Thomas thought about the Cathars, who were dualists and condemned matter as emanating from the principle of evil. This explains why they refused the Eucharist, because it includes matter, bread and wine: this whole episode is telling.

17 In a more or less dualistic view, the only value of matter is to be the occasion for a transfer, as a kind of envelope that will serve no further purpose. If, on the contrary, we give matter its density, the sacramental balance will be greatly changed, and we will see operate a completely different Platonism than that of Augustine: that of the Greek doctors, the Cappadocians, Gregory of Nyssa, Dionysius, and Maximus. They reintroduced into their Platonism the high value of matter, either by adopting, as Maximus does, Aristotelian foundations, or above all because they saw the realism of the incarnation. Maximus's anti-monophysitism and anti-monothelitism play out in all sectors: incarnation, sacramental order, Church realities, creation recapitulated down to matter, while, even if going further than Augustine, the Augustinians of the Middle Ages liquidated matter to arrive at the perfect world; these Greeks say that there is no perfect world if there is no matter.

18 The emanation from God—and for thirteenth century scholasticism the word "emanate" does not have the pejorative meaning it has now—the emanating flow of creation, takes place by degrees of being. Each degree engages the other, and this emanation goes as far as matter, but, in the ascent to God, each level, in its being and in its epistemology, is alleged only insofar as it tends to the rung above: matter tends to plant life, plant life to animal life, animal

life to human life, human life to divine life. Each being has its own density only insofar as it is open to the above, in a dynamic of "participation," according to the philosophical term to which corresponds the Dionysian axiom "supremum infimi tangit infimum supremi": the summit of promotion of a being opens up to the level of being higher without it being able to enter there, at the same time as the lower level of this other level meets the lower reality.

Multiplicity of Levels and Unity

19 There is a kind of spiral, and this multiplicity of levels coordinates in unity, according to the metaphysics of the One, characteristic of neoplatonism. Thus, in each level of being, there is a reciprocal attraction which constitutes the universe, not through layered superimpositions, which would be very Aristotelian, but in that each level tends to gain the other and the other influences to promote, while reserving autonomy, the property of the lower level. Of itself it tends to the higher level in a reciprocal attraction, a tension between the intelligible world of the spirit and the sensible world of phenomena.

20 The medievals found in Dionysius's *Celestial Hierarchy* this ontology of participation. Stripped of the oriental imagery of the nine choirs of angels, we will consider the notion of hierarchy for its own sake, stripping it of any imaginative representation. The essence of the Dionysian notion lies in this tension which reconciles the idea of hierarchical ordering of beings with the fundamental relationship between God and the world: it is analogy. I was thinking about this yesterday in connection with the agonizing problem of transcendence and immanence. I am quite incapable of solving it and I have no soothing answer, but I believe that we have in Dionysian thought a deep perception to properly pose the problem, apart from Augustinianism such as it is still in Blondel. In an emanentist conception of the universe, with tensions at each level, I understand much better how God is immanent in matter, and yet matter and the human being are open ontologically by the natural desire to see God. The starting position seems much better to me; but unfortunately, it has remained alien to theology.

21 Look at Maximus's anthropology: the growth of beings is accomplished in union, without suppressing the autonomy of each. The material universe has an authentic density under and through the creative presence of God. There again we meet St. Thomas. Things *are*; they have their own density, they are and they are good, and not simply by reference to the supreme Goodness, external to themselves. Moreover, their goodness is the "cause" of their reference. The emanation from God causes them to have being; their reference to God is subsequent to their existence, according to a paradoxical logical analysis proposed by St. Thomas.

22 Thus the sensible world has its full ontological value, through this role of being the phenomenon of the spirit, while the spirit, for its part, reveals itself fully in this material mirror, in no way provisional, but eternal and definitive. Thus there is a perfect circumincession (*perichoresis*) of the spiritual world and the sensible world. The world is one: the intelligible world in its totality appears phenomenally in the totality of the sensible world, mystically expressed by symbolic images, for the eyes which can see. The whole sensible world is immanent in the whole intelligible world; in the former by reason, in the latter by *symbols*, and the work of the two is one. Intelligibility is the soul of the sensible, as the body of the intelligible is the sensible. The intelligible world is no less immanent in the sensible world than the soul is in the body; the sensible world is sensitive to the intelligible world like the body forged by the soul. Unique cosmos, like the consubstantiality of body and soul constitutes the unique person, without either of the two elements suppressing or repudiating the other.

23 This anthropology of Maximus, the description of which I literally borrow from Fr. Urs von Balthasar,[7] has not been fully developed in the anthropology of St. Thomas, but it appears here and there. In the thirteenth century, where several recent translations of Dionysius circulated, a Dionysian corpus of masters from the University of Paris was formed, with a Dionysius wrapped in

7. Translators' note: That is, Hans Urs von Balthasar. Chenu appears to have in mind works such as Hans Urs von Balthasar, *Cosmic Liturgy: The Universe according to Maximus the Confessor* (San Francisco: Ignatius Press, 2003).

glosses which came precisely from Maximus and Scotus Eriugena, and a set of data already elaborated, reworked, purged of the Orientalism of Dionysius. Albert the Great and Thomas Aquinas read these amalgamated texts; we even have, by the hand of St. Thomas, the reportage of Albert the Great's lectures on the Divine Names. We speak of the entry of Aristotle; I also want to speak of the entry of Dionysius, which saturated the atmosphere, as the thesis of Fr. Emilio Garcia will show.

Humanity and the Cosmos

24 We have here a cultural phenomenon which goes far beyond the critical analysis of Dionysius's text and which touches the whole anthropology of St. Thomas. The human person recapitulates the cosmos in themself. They are at the junction of matter and spirit, the pivot through which all matter is recapitulated in them; they humanize matter, and thus matter is deified. By humanizing the world, the human person takes possession of it according to the way of creation, and this is how it is deified. So much so that in order to be perfect and perfectly blessed, the human being needs matter; for at that time I will possess my complete nature, and by possessing it I will be nearer to God. The closer I take possession of my material nature, the closer I will be to the spiritual. Matter thus plays a direct part in my beatitude. The separated soul is badly assimilated to God.[8]

25 This tension, this reciprocal attraction, this progressive constitution of the cosmos, this energy of which humanity is the recapitulating pivot, has its noetic expression in the *symbol*. The symbol is not the effect of a transfer of meaning beyond matter; it is the very articulation of the density of matter which retains its totality of being instead of being glossed over by the spirit. This is why the mystery, in all creation, is present through symbolic play to the point that when this economy of tension, of attraction, of circumincession, is consumed, there will be such a deep embedding of matter in the mind that there will be no more need for

8. Cf. Thomas Aquinas, *De Potentia*, q. 5, a. 10, ad 5 (and co).

symbols anymore: humanity will be accomplished. The totality of matter will be invested in the totality of the spirit.

26 Before Adam's sin—with all the mythical aspects of medieval theologies of Adam—humanity was perfect: at that time there were no sacraments, and the human being was such that the whole of their mind was in the totality of matter. There was no need for the attraction I mentioned. It is archeology, you will say, what does this have to do with pastoral ministry of the sacraments? I answer that it is the subsoil that must fuel our symbolic reflection and make concrete the importance of the visible symbol.

27 Let us confront this with the Augustinian categories as practiced by scholasticism, and more especially with the notion of *sign*. The signpost on the road is the indicator of a region. The sign is a procedure of the mind which unconsciously involves a depreciation of matter, which is only a means instead of being an original density. When I speak of significations, there is no longer the Dionysian descent, this manifestation and this presence of things according to the continuity which is the logic of this descent, according to the Platonic logic of participation. I consulted Karl Rahner's theological dictionary for the word "symbol."[9] For him the sign (I have some difficulty in dissociating *symbol* and *sign* because, whatever I do, I am Augustinian) is an element arbitrarily chosen by the human being and put outwardly in relation to a given reality to signal its presence in time and space. The symbol, on the other hand, is a "manifestation": it is the symbolized reality itself which, to varying degrees, asserts itself in a reality that is at the same time different and joint, and therefore at the same time exteriorizes and expresses itself in it. We are literally in another universe which takes shape in the semantic density of the word *symbol*.

28 In Augustine, this notion of sign is linked to his very mentality, more than to a theory. For him, the interior is the place of the truth. We can schematize his route of conversion as the passage from fantasies to truth. Discovered thanks to Neoplatonism, though a particular Neoplatonism, the truth is interior and, insofar as it

9. Translators' note: i.e., "Symbol," in Karl Rahner and Herbert Vorgrimler, *Concise Theological Dictionary* (London: Burns & Oates, 1983), 491.

remains subject to the exterior, it is still crippled. This implies as a second movement that the soul can reside in the truth only if it is delivered from the flesh, if it is autonomous to find pure interiority. The flesh diverts the will from its true good. It comprises an inside and an outside, at its summit interiority is pure interiority. This is why the world is only a parafunction.

29 We therefore have two couples, the pair *symbol* and *mystery*, and the pair *signum* and *res*, which Peter Lombard detached from Augustine's ensemble to make it the fundamental category of all theology, which studies two things: the *res* and the *signa*. These Augustinian-inspired categories introduce and govern the problem of causality. It is to try to see the articulation between *signum* and *res* that we introduce the word cause: these signs are causes. Introducing this very determined philosophical vocabulary creates a serious problem, which distressed St. Bonaventure.[10] St. Bonaventure is an occasionalist: matter is an opportunity; it is God who confers grace, not matter. St. Thomas says: yes. He introduces the philosophical notion of "instrumental" cause which is, I think, a very rich concept. But there is a crisis over the word "cause." In reality, this category is unsuited for making intelligible the relation between the two levels described earlier, which are intelligible by analogy, whereas the philosophical "cause" is made for the explanation of a homogeneous world, that is, one that is "unequivocal," as the logicians used to say. It is at a determined epistemological level that the causes play out and we cannot, through a cause of one level, explain another. If I want to explain my psychological game by biological phenomena, there is a part of the truth, but I cannot explain the phenomenon of the higher level by the causality of the lower, or by matter the vegetal level or the psychological. It is the error of sociologists or psychologists when they want to explain, by such a reduction, the summits of human life.

30 The two levels that I described earlier are reconnected by analogy, which finds its expression in the *symbol*. I am not saying that the concept of *cause* does not explain, but we could compare it to

10. Cf. the texts indicated by Pierre-Marie Gy, "Problèmes de théologie sacramentaire," *La Maison-Dieu* 110 (1972): 129–42 (141 n29).

a screwdriver by which we would like to replace the key that opens a door; it is made for something else. Let us add, by allusion to the present philosophical concept, that the ontology of causality is today, rightly or wrongly, evanescent. Nowadays an intelligent person, even a practicing one, has difficulty understanding a sacramental causal analysis. The cause cannot be a dogmatic concept of permanent efficacy, even if it should not be denied all intelligibility. On the contrary, the way is clear for the role of intelligibility of the symbol. In other words, I am led to a critique of Augustinian sacramentalism as linked to a "spiritualist" anthropology in which matter is devitalized from its symbolic capacity.

31 According to the biblical mode of thinking, the human being must be considered in all their concrete reality, purged of any dualism in the oppositions between soul and body, spirit and matter—and I would add, by telescoping the analyses, between history and cosmos, and even between grace and nature. As you know, *Gaudium et Spes* expressly ruled out a dualism between grace and nature. Unfortunately, we see in the commentaries that everyone has reintroduced it without thinking about it. It is not that the distinction is without analytical value, but it is insufficient to grasp reality as it is, both that of salvation and that of human density. A similar observation would be made about a dualism between creation and incarnation; the sin of sacramental Augustinianism in scholasticism is to leave aside creation, when instead the incarnation must find its full value in it.

32 I read with complacency an article by H. Denis, in which he expresses the fear that Moltmann's philosophy of the future—at least in his first work—might obscure a certain reality of the cosmos.[11] H. Denis wonders if Christianity should so quickly eliminate the "epiphanic dimension of the world," the epiphanic dimension of creation, that is to say its aptitude to manifest the presence of God recapitulated in Jesus Christ. Otherwise one could wonder if the Church would not be frustrated with a certain sacramental dimension. In sacramentality, we find again the junction of the

11. Translators' note: Chenu refers here to Henri Denis, sometime professor at the seminary at Lyon and *peritus* at Vatican II.

cosmos and history. Instead of only the incarnation being the sacramental source, it is also already the cosmos itself, and unity is reestablished with creation, which is somehow still in progress, and where I am a partner of God.

33 Yesterday we mentioned those who rediscovered the epiphanic dimension of the liturgy, like Romano Guardini, or Cipriano Vagaggini, in the footsteps of the Greek Fathers. I would add, for this sensibility of vision which characterizes him: Teilhard de Chardin. Without realizing it, we breathe it in. Against the myth of St. Gregory the Great according to which God created human beings to replace fallen angels and imitate the angelic liturgy, I prefer the cosmic liturgy, where matter enters because it is assumed by the spirit. I need matter so that creation enters into the play of the liturgy and is not left out. Rituality implies this, and spiritual worship will be fully spirit when matter is in it, and not when removed.

34 Let us return to our starting point: geared towards an anthropology, theological rationality confers on the mystery, or rather on the sacrament, a complete coherence with human realism. In other words, the whole of the mystery, including its sacramentality, finds its realism starting from the human being. Against all spiritualisms, the total being of the human; against individualisms, the social being; against the external cosmos, the human master of the world. I challenge philosophical Augustinianism for its theology and its internalizing spirituality. I am thinking here of the *Imitation of Christ,* which nourished generations, including in the nineteenth century and the beginning of the twentieth. When I was in seminary, I read it every day. An admirable booklet, the limits of which I feel today. In this complete interiority, the world no longer exists, while the totality of creation must enter into the totality of the spirit. I said this bluntly, whereas it would take a lot of discernment. I wanted to shake your drowsy Augustinianism.

Part Two

Seven Essays by Contemporary Scholars

A Faith That Holds to the Body

Olivier Praud

In today's context, thinking about the way in which human action and God's action interact in the liturgy seems radically necessary. Different cultures have different ways of celebrating the Christian mystery, reflecting their conception of the believer. In a caricatured way, the liturgy often seems to be torn between a demand for the sacred and a desire to reach out to the concrete lives of participants. The first one relies on a coefficient of strangeness brought to its maximum in the gestures, vestments, and words in order to better manifest the transcendent dimension of the liturgical action. The second one, on the other hand, seeks to make room for sensitive signs and even for a certain creativity in order to integrate new words and gestures capable of bearing witness to God's place in the lives of all people. One might think that it would be enough to find a middle way to resolve this conflict.

However, the theology of the liturgy cannot be satisfied with this. If the liturgy is indeed the mirror of the representations that structure our vision of human beings, it resists all forms of dualism. In contemporary hypermodernity, humanity finds itself at the heart of multiple tensions: technicality vs. spiritualism, liberalism vs. normativity, cancel culture vs. historicism. As a result, to quote *Desiderio Desideravi*, Gnosticism and Pelagianism are finding new forms that undermine the way in which liturgical participation can be "the primary and indispensable source from which the faithful are to derive the true Christian spirit."[1] Through its very celebration, the liturgy maps

1. *Desiderio Desideravi* 16–17, https://www.vatican.va/content/francesco/en/apost_letters/documents/20220629-lettera-ap-desiderio-desideravi.html; *Sacrosanctum*

out an itinerary where the most spiritual and the most corporeal are united. Every gesture, word, and movement becomes a sign of salvation through which God offers grace as a gift. In the Eucharist, the gesture of breaking bread remains decisive. It is not reduced to its functional dimension, which is necessary if everyone is to share in eucharistic communion. Not only does it fulfill what was announced in the consecration, "Jesus took bread, said the blessing, broke it and gave it to his disciples," but it also fulfills what Christ's life is: a gift from God for the salvation of the world. The liturgy's capacity to resist does not lie in a simple epistemological shift. It lies in an anthropology renewed from within by the mystery of the incarnation.

This is what drives Chenu's approach. By advocating, in his time, for a sacramental anthropology, he noted that sacramental theology was overwhelmingly based on a spiritualist conception of the human being. As a result, the sacrament is understood as a sensitive sign that makes visible a hidden intelligible reality. Matter, reduced to a sign pointing to that which transcends it, is thus discredited and its capacity to mediate is altered. In concrete liturgical action, Chenu identifies a proposal for overcoming this hiatus. By proposing in several articles a renewed hermeneutic of the sacramental vision of Thomas Aquinas, the Dominican from Le Saulchoir invites us to start afresh from human realism, from an anthropology which upholds the principle of "the radical co-naturality of the sensible in the sacramental economy."[2]

Also, read again the "liturgical and sacramental" contributions of Chenu offer an opportunity to draw on the source of a reflection that inscribes God's entry into history as the bearing condition of all theology. Chenu's realism of the incarnation permeates his thinking on the historicity of theology and the Word of God, as well as the historical practice of the church as a theological site. By indicating that "we can only engage the sacrament in consubstantiality with the human" and that "'anthropology' and 'sacramental' are inseparable from each other,"[3] he invites us to consider corporeality as the starting point for any theology of the liturgy. We must therefore begin by understanding

Concilium 14, https://www.vatican.va/archive/hist_councils/ii_vatican_council/documents/vat-ii_const_19631204_sacrosanctum-concilium_en.html.

2. Chenu 1974, par. 15

3. Chenu 1974, par. 5.

the way in which Chenu considers this condition proper to humanity. Secondly, it will be possible to identify some of its characteristics for sacramental reflection on humanity's situation. Finally, the interest of re-reading Chenu for an anthropological theology of the sacraments will be highlighted.

A "Naturalistic" Approach

Drawing on a careful reading of Aquinas, Chenu wants to start again from the sacramental fact itself. There is sacramentality because of the very nature of human condition and, even more, because of the divine will that provides each reality according to its own mode of being. Matter cannot be rejected as in a Platonic approach. It permeates the very mystery of salvation: "The sacramental order is in physical continuity with the economy of mystery."[4] Also, the corporeality attached to the sacrament makes possible the path where humanity can tend to the knowledge of intelligible things by means of sensible things. For Thomas Aquinas, it is through matter that humanity will be divinized. Matter possesses a real consistency that is capable of linking sign and meaning. Following Aquinas, Chenu maintains that the raison d'être of a sacrament is not primarily to be a remedy, but because the human being is equipped with senses and it is through a corporeal and sensory itinerary that humanity can be led to salvation.

This vision is based on a "naturalistic"[5] approach, developed in his own way by Thomas Aquinas, and which Chenu sees as the beginnings of anthropological integration. Between his *Summa contra Gentiles* and his *Summa Theologica,* Aquinas shifts his focus to the very nature of the human being.[6] Already, by considering the sacraments as a remedy, he is taking into account the concrete condition of humanity in its sinfulness: wounded in their relationship to matter, they need a remedy that goes as far as the materiality of existence to heal and restore them to a reconciled relationship with the world. Similarly, by linking the seven sacraments to the different stages of human life and

4. Chenu 1952, par. 8.

5. Chenu 1974, par. 9.

6. Jean-Baptiste Metz, *L'homme anthropocentrique chrétienne - Pour une interprétation ouverte de la philosophie de saint Thomas* (Paris: Mame, 1968).

its growth, Thomas once again aims to inscribe sacramentality in the pivotal moments of the individual or the human community. Thus, for Chenu, a form of parallelism emerges between the corporal life and the spiritual life. The spiritualization and humanization of human beings progress together, enabling them to render true worship to God (Rom 12:1). For him, this is also a sign that all sacramentality is rooted in an anthropological soil that is, in a way, its grammar. "If the sacrament is first of all matter, the way I conceive of matter will modify my understanding of the sacrament: either matter in itself, or matter in the cosmos, or of the matter in the human being, the body."[7]

For Aquinas, taking the path of the sensible and the corporeal is still the guarantee of a vision of the sacraments that does not fall into a dualism in which matter is merely a vehicle of grace. For this reason, by adopting instrumental causality to characterize the sacramental process, he demonstrates to the highest degree the inescapable part played by humanity and its corporeality in the whole process. This is underpinned by the capacity of matter to lead from one step to the next to a participation in the divine being. Inherited from the anthropology of Maximus the Confessor, according to Chenu, this participation highlights how the human being occupies a cardinal place at the frontier between matter and spirit, the sensible and the intelligible. He humanizes the world, and in this way the world can be divinized. The sacrament accomplishes in a singular way in the human being what they are called to achieve by their very existence.

In such a sacramental "realism," the human body is called upon to play a singular role. Taking up the fundamental intuitions of the sacramentary of Thomas Aquinas, Chenu sets out to give full consistency to the material and, by extension, to the gestures and words of the liturgy and their implementation in the sacramental celebration. To introduce people to the heart of God's love, God takes the path that makes it possible to participate fully and totally in that love. This is not a concession, but the need to re-evaluate the liturgical instance in a sacramental theology whose epistemological matrix made it secondary. As a result, the liturgy must give the body its rightful place, with all its individual and collective components, in order to "be *true* in

7. Chenu 1974, par. 16.

humanity."[8] And this is a fundamental characteristic that bears witness to the fact that humanity can only be humanity because they are in the world. Their concrete situation is to be inscribed in the cosmos, in time and in history, and to be there not only as an individual, but also as a human community:

> geared towards an anthropology, theological rationality confers on the mystery, or rather on the sacrament, a complete coherence with human realism. In other words, the whole of the mystery, including its sacramentality, finds its realism starting from the human being. Against all spiritualisms, the total being of the human; against individualisms, the social being; against the external cosmos, the human master of the world.[9]

Recourse to anthropology is therefore the only way to build a sacramentary that links its point of departure and its point of arrival, humanity and God. If the human sciences are called upon to form part of theological reflection, this goes beyond a simple ancillary use. Without succumbing to an anthropological reduction, they constitute from the outset the means of integrating the believing person as a principle at the heart of all theology and, in particular, that of the sacraments and the liturgy.

The Body as a Human "Situation"

According to Chenu, being corporeal and therefore subject to temporality are two characteristics of humanity that mark their earthly activities. There is a good reason historical research is a constant theme in his work. On the one hand, he constantly endeavours to situate the evolutions and variations of dogmatic statements throughout their construction, the better to highlight how they are an expression of the church's unchanging faith. On the other hand, he is aware of the extent to which the church must discern the "signs of the times" not according to a mundane logic of progress, but according to the

8. Chenu 1967, par. 18.
9. Chenu 1974, par. 34.

fundamental orientation of human life as it awaits full communion with God. His contributions at the origin of this book bear witness to this. By theologically considering liturgy and sacrament from an anthropology returned to its origins, and in which the human body represents the point of insertion, it is then possible to outline a path of salvation at the very heart of humanity. The history of salvation cannot simply be the end of human history, nor can it be radically external to it. If it is to be consistent with divine salvation, it must be the very fabric of human history. By restoring to matter its dual characteristics of sensible reality and meaning, Chenu leads us to situate corporeality as the supporting condition of all divine work.

As a perfect reader of Thomas Aquinas, he began by restoring to the corporeal the ontological density it had lost in the momentum of a certain medieval Augustinianism. Driven by a subtle rejection of the materiality of humanity and of what constitutes them, the latter saw it only as a transitory state. In contrast, Chenu defends the consubstantiality between body and spirit, which enables human beings to unify what they are externally and internally. In so doing, corporeality is given its rightful place in a unitive understanding of humanity.[10] Soul and body are not separate realities, but two facets of the same reality: "the human being must be considered in all their concrete reality, purged of any dualism in the oppositions between soul and body, spirit and matter—and I would add, by telescoping the analyses, between history and cosmos, and even between grace and nature."[11]

Rejecting all dualism, he sees humanity as an alliance in which matter and spirit are consubstantial, that is, in which one contributes to the reality of the other and *vice versa*. Spirit and matter determine each other and are therefore not two separate things linked by a cause-and-effect relationship. As a result, soul and body are intimately united. Just as the soul is nothing without its body, so the body is nothing without being animated through and through: "not two things, not a soul having a body or moving a body, but an incarnated soul, an animated body . . . spirit and matter allow each other to exist; they

10. Chenu 1947, par. 5.
11. Chenu 1974, par. 31.

mutually constitute, sustain, and determine one another."[12] In this way, the body is not an obstacle to the sanctification of human beings but a *sine qua non* condition. Nor is it a temporary state from which we must detach ourselves. It opens the way for humanity to participate fully in God's salvation. Our intelligence contemplates God and the world through the same gaze, both spiritual and material. This requires an understanding in which anthropology and theology are in fruitful dialogue: "If matter in every sense of the word, *res sensibilis* and, for us, the human body, is the first essential component of the sacrament, an intelligibility different from matter will influence the understanding of the sacrament."[13]

For the theologian from Le Saulchoir, nothing is sacred in the Christian system, but everything is to be consecrated. The body plays a cardinal role in this process. The merit of his approach lies precisely in linking this consecration to a human who is fully understood. He received from the Angelic Doctor a vision of the human person that "recapitulates the cosmos in themself."[14] By uniting matter and spirit, he humanizes matter and thus makes its divinization possible. Consequently, the body is humanity's "situation,"[15] the interface of its condition in history and the cosmos. First of all, the body enables the divine mystery to unfold in time and to reach out to people throughout the ages. The reiteration of the liturgy is the means of concretely unfolding the paschal mystery of Christ's death and resurrection, accomplished once and for all so that it reaches all people. The time of the sacrament combines the past event on which it is based, the present day in which it is celebrated, and its fulfillment in all its fullness. In this way, the mystery is made present, not as a reminder of a past event, but as the salvation we experience today and which commits us to the

12. Marie-Dominique Chenu, *Aquinas and His Role in Theology* trans. Paul Philibert (Collegeville, MN : Liturgical Press, 2002), 93.

13. Chenu 1974, par. 16.

14. Chenu 1974, par. 24.

15. Marie-Dominique Chenu, "Situation humaine, corporalité et temporalité," in *La Parole de Dieu*, vol. 2: *L'Évangile dans le temps*, 411–36 (Paris: Éd. du Cerf, "Cogitatio Fidei" 11, 1964); ET: Chenu, "The Human Situation: Corporeality and Temporality," in *Faith and Theology*, 116–36 (Dublin: M.H. Gill and Son, 1968).

future.[16] Then, this being-body concretely translates humanity's presence to itself, to others, and to the world. The human condition unfolds through the mediations and things that surround us. So, our corporeality radically inscribes our presence with God in God's presence with the world. The two are intimately linked. They are not relative, but ordered one to the other, one by the other. Chenu's thinking aims to restore a theandric density to all liturgical activity. The human-divine alliance of the liturgy is not by default, but by excess.

Finally, this unitive vision finds its fulfillment in the communitarian perspective of the liturgy. The human body is not considered first and foremost individually but is always already inscribed in the Mystical Body that is the church. Hence the need for active participation that builds it up and makes it manifest:

> The liturgy [is] essentially communal because it expresses the essentially social nature of humanity in the Mystical Body of Christ. Since it assumes the human requests and resources of the Christian community in prayer, the liturgy implies, confirms, and consecrates an anthropology. . . . At the same time, one can imagine, the liturgy finds in this science of humanity its openness to the current world, as well as its capacity to sacramentalize in its "ceremonies" certain activities typical of contemporary human beings.[17]

For Chenu, the liturgy is necessarily communitarian for the reason that it expresses, in the Mystical Body of Christ, the essentially social nature of humanity. In return, this sociality is transformed to express itself in communion and charity. Social commitment, which was like a counterpoint at the heart of his Dominican ministry, fulfills the sacramental aim and its concrete roots.

Toward the Sacramentality of Becoming a Christian?

For Chenu, the liturgy and the sacraments are part of the "spiritual economy" of communicating the mystery and knowing it. The theologian from Le Saulchoir regrets that the anthropological and symbolic

16. Chenu 1952, par. 23–24.
17. Chenu 1947, par. 1–2.

approach is minimized, or even rejected, because it is considered to be pre-theological:

> The matter . . . remains the living flesh of sacramentalism. It is distressing to see how too often it is brought back to pseudo-philosophical categories, where, by an undue transfer of Aristotelian hylomorphism, the pre-theological character of the symbolic game is eliminated.[18]

This regret, expressed in 1947, retains its relevance in view of the difficulties of developing a theological reflection on the liturgy from an anthropological foundation. By restoring the body to its rightful place within a theology of the sacraments, in the light of the achievements of the anthropological sciences, it is possible to better perceive how the sacramental cannot remain within a productionist or subjectivist logic of grace. Because the body is the locus of all human relationships, whether sensitive or situational, rational or spiritual, we need to integrate the human process of grace into theological reflection itself. By reweaving the links between mystery, sacrament, and anthropology, Chenu invites us to sketch out several perspectives on the sacramentality of Christian becoming.

The first one is the need to re-evaluate rituality as the place and time where the most spiritual and the most corporeal are articulated. Chenu's analysis invites us to better grasp how rituality is appropriate and homogeneous to the mystery itself. Within the sacramental economy of revelation, the "composite of words and actions,"[19] and thus that of the body, allows the mystery to unfold at a human level. Human realities thus become capable of allowing us to contemplate divine life itself. Is it not so the case when, at the beginning of the Easter Vigil, the paschal candle illuminates the darkened nave with the light of the resurrection? Through the ritual dynamic, the symbol is brought to the point of incandescence, the better to manifest the victory of the risen Lord. The link between mystery and symbol is not pure unveiling or veiling. But the to-and-fro between the two allows the divine mystery to remain itself, a reality that is always to be received and deciphered at the

18. Chenu 1947, par. 16.
19. Chenu 1952, par. 18.

very heart of human existence. Through its symbolic texture, rituality thus offers the liturgy a way of welcoming the mystery and making it present, while respecting its own nature: at once unfathomable truth and yet knowable, a total gift and yet always to be received. The dogmatic scope of rituality is thus a form of hermeneutics, of intelligence and participation in the very reality to which it leads us.

Secondly, for Chenu, corporeality irreducibly carries with it a collective dimension. Liturgy is communal by nature, and not the sum of the persons present. If we are to develop a sufficiently consistent theology of the liturgy, we need to start again with the assembly. All too often, this theology takes as its starting point the believing subject and expands from strength to strength to gain its ecclesiological scope. "These symbolic actions appear, develop, and multiply in collective bodies: communities of the Christian people where the participants are actors and not just spectators."[20] Consequently, we need to reverse the way in which the *actuosa participatio* is often understood. Active participation is not at the service of group facilitation. By ritually articulating the inner assent of faith and its outer expression, it enables each person to discover that he or she is part of a tradition of faith, a *traditio fidei*. They see themselves linked to their brothers and sisters in the faith who pray with them, but also to those who have gone before them, to those who are absent, and to those who will succeed them in the faith. Because it is at the service of an epiphany of the covenant of individual bodies in the Mystical Body of the church, inseparably the Body of Christ, the people of God, and the temple of the Spirit, this participation flourishes as communion, as *caritas*. Becoming a Christian is radically about becoming in God with others.

A final research perspective concerns the relationship between theology and the human sciences. Chenu rejects an anthropology that does not give matter, and in this case the human body, its proper density. By highlighting the limits of the scholastic interpretation of Augustinian sacramentalism, which devalued matter in favor of a spiritualist approach, Chenu aims to give space to the symbolic capacity of matter in its ability to manifest the presence of God. "I need matter so that creation enters into the play of the liturgy and is not left out.

20. Chenu 1947, par. 12.

Rituality implies this, and spiritual worship will be fully spirit when matter is in it, and not when removed."[21] The corporeality of faith requires a strong interdisciplinary approach, as evoked in the *proemium* of *Veritatis gaudium*: "a cross-disciplinary, situating and stimulating all disciplines against the backdrop of the Light and Life offered by the Wisdom streaming from God's Revelation" (4c). This corporeality can represent a forum for dialogue between epistemologies. To put it another way, it is a question of creating a theology that is thoroughly anthropological, by virtue of the realism of the incarnation that the history of salvation and of becoming Christian presuppose.

In conclusion, Chenu's thought remains stimulating because it forces us to question the way in which the theology of the sacraments and the liturgy has taken into account the best of the anthropological turn of the twentieth century. By integrating the anthropological meaning of liturgical actions in a way that is not contradictory to the theological meaning, it is possible to create a sacramentary that integrates the way in which people become believers. The realism of the incarnation defended by Chenu leads us to pursue the anthropological turn in theology. Honoring the corporeality of the liturgy and sacramental rituality, based on its concrete conditions, is a way of developing a theology of the liturgy that redraws the unity between dogma, spirituality, Sacred Scripture, and pastoral ministry. This approach finds a singular echo in Pope Francis's letter on liturgical formation, *Desiderio Desideravi*. It outlines the challenge we must take up if we are to have a liturgy at the service of a faith that embraces the body:

> The Liturgy does not leave us alone to search out an individual supposed knowledge of the mystery of God. Rather, it takes us by the hand, together, as an assembly, to lead us deep within the mystery that the Word and the sacramental signs reveal to us. And it does this, consistent with all action of God, following the way of the Incarnation, that is, by means of the symbolic language of the body, which extends to things in space and time. (DD 19)

21. Chenu 1974, par. 33.

Liturgical Theology as Fundamental Theology

Stephan van Erp

Can liturgy be regarded as revelational? If so, what is the relationship and division of tasks between liturgical theology and fundamental theology? In this chapter, I will discuss Chenu's texts on the liturgy in view of these questions. I hope to contribute to current discussions in liturgical theology, but also to provide a new perspective on the work of Chenu, commonly appreciated for its significance in the development of twentieth-century historical Thomism and the theology of labor. Reading Chenu as a fundamental theologian, however, will make manifest that he has been a distinct voice in the *ressourcement* tradition of thought. *Ressourcement* theology has gained new interest in contemporary theology, but rarely features Chenu as one of its main protagonists.[1] By taking liturgy as a starting point, I will show that the theoretical and methodological reflections of fundamental theology are deeply rooted in liturgical practice. In his articles on liturgy, however, Chenu proceeds in the opposite direction to show that in order to understand liturgical practices, one needs fundamental

1. With some exceptions, for example: Jon Kirwan, *An Avant-garde Theological Generation: The Nouvelle Théologie and the French Crisis of Modernity* (Oxford: Oxford University Press, 2018); Patricia Kelly, ed., *Ressourcement Theology: A Sourcebook* (London: T&T Clark, 2021); and Sarah Shortall, *Soldiers of God in a Secular World: Catholic Theology and Twentieth-Century French Politics* (Cambridge, MA: Harvard University Press, 2021).

theology to explain their revelatory and sacramental qualities. In other words, he believes a fundamental theology of the liturgy undergirds liturgical theology. But does that also entail that liturgical theology is a fundamental theology?

In what follows, I will first discuss the absence of liturgy in the development of modern fundamental theology. Despite the commonly accepted claim that liturgy is a *locus theologicus*, it is conspicuously absent as a theme in the field of fundamental theology. Recent liturgical theology, however, presents itself quite explicitly as a *theologia prima*. Next, I will discuss the sources that shaped Chenu's theology of liturgy, especially the Dominican influences on his ideas of contemplation and sacraments. Then, I will use his thoughts on liturgy to reconstruct his liturgical theology as a fundamental theology. I hope to show that Chenu could be a good conversation partner in current discussions on the idea of liturgy as revelation.

An Invisible Source: Liturgy in Fundamental Theology

Reading Chenu's texts on liturgy from the viewpoint of fundamental theology opens up new perspectives on his work, but not before one is confronted with the limits of such an approach. Fundamental theology offers no common ground for reflections on liturgy. There is also a sharp contrast between the developments of fundamental theology and liturgical theology. Whereas the former seems to have come to a standstill, the latter seems to thrive in contemporary theology. Moreover, the two fields of study seem to focus their attention on quite distinct objects, and especially fundamental theology turns out to have a blind spot for everything liturgical, while liturgical theology has been paying more attention to foundational matters.

A glance at the field of fundamental theology proper will show that the theme of liturgy is conspicuously absent. In René Latourelle and Rino Fisichella's *Dizzionario di Teologia Fondamentale*, there is no mention of liturgy, and no reference to the sacraments either.[2] Interestingly, the term "liturgy" would have come before the lemma on *loci theologici*. Even under that heading, liturgy is not mentioned,

2. René Latourelle and Rino Fisichella, eds., *Dizzionario di Teologia Fondamentale* (Assisi: Cittadella Editrice, 1990).

but the reason for this is that the description is limited to Melchior Cano's *loci*, which do not encompass liturgy either. In the German fundamental theological tradition, for example in Heinrich Fries's *Fundamentaltheologie*, or Hans Waldenfels's *Kontextuelle Fundamentaltheologie*, both from the 1980s, there is almost no mention of liturgy (or "Gottesdienst"). It is referenced in passing in the third demonstration on the church, the *demonstratio catholica*, as part of the description of the structure of the church and its authority.[3] In more recent works of fundamental theology, for example in Perry Schmidt-Leukel's *Grundkurs Fundamentaltheologie* or Jürgen Werbick's *Den Glauben verantworten*, again, there is no mention of liturgy.[4] Werbick does dedicate a section on the church as sacrament in what he calls "der Streitfall Kirche," so it really depends on how much one would allow the notion of the liturgical to also encompass the sacramental in the broadest ecclesiological sense, to be able to conclude that there is at least some attention to liturgy in German fundamental theology. In a more recent work by Markus Knapp, who tries to rationally account for theological metaphysics in postmodern times, the attention has completely shifted to the plausibility of theological epistemology, which has no place for the particularities and idiosyncrasies of the Catholic liturgy.[5]

In Anglo-American theology, the situation is much the same. In the work of perhaps the best-known fundamental theologian of recent decades, the Jesuit Gerald O'Collins, there is no extensive treatment of liturgical practices, but with some imagination it could be found in his presentation of the biblical canon as a foundation of theology.[6] O'Collins follows Karl Rahner's theory of the formation of the

3. Heinrich Fries, *Fundamentaltheologie* (Graz, Vienna, Cologne: Verlag Styria, 1985); Hans Waldenfels, *Kontextuelle Fundamentaltheologie* (Paderborn: Ferdinand Schöningh, 1988).

4. Perry Schmidt-Leukel, *Grundkurs Fundamentaltheologie: Eine Einführung in die Grundfragen des christlichten Glaubens* (München: Don Bosco Verlag, 1999); Jürgen Werbick, *Den Glauben verantworten: Eine Fundamentaltheologie* (Freiburg im Breisgau: Herder, 2000).

5. Markus Knapp, *Die Vernunft des Glaubens: Einführung in die Fundamentaltheologie* (Freiburg im Breisgau: Herder, 2009).

6. Gerald O'Collins, SJ, *Rethinking Fundamental Theology* (Oxford: Oxford University Press, 2011), 216–33.

canon, understood as deeply rooted in the liturgy of the early church. O'Collins identifies the canon as "original" revelation, so in as far as the liturgy has shaped it, he seems to leave some place for the foundational role of the liturgy in the history of faith and theology, and in the recognition of the holiness of the Scriptures. One might, perhaps, expect more attention to liturgy in *Fundamental Theology*, by the Benedictine Guy Mansini, whose work is influenced by Joseph Ratzinger, who saw the liturgy as a foundational theological theme, but again, the liturgy does not feature in it.[7]

Based on this first heuristic journey along some of the most influential introductions and handbooks of fundamental theology from the past few decades, one can conclude that there is a noticeable lack of attention to the liturgy. Fundamental theologians today are therefore faced with a serious challenge: Should liturgical practices be addressed as a foundation of faith or as an expression of ongoing revelation? Should liturgy be a prominent theme in fundamental theology, next to faith and reason, revelation and Christ, and tradition and the church? Perhaps it should even be considered as a fourth demonstration—besides the *demonstratio religiosa*, the *demonstratio christiana*, and the *demonstratio catholica*—of the coherence and legitimacy of the Christian faith, a *demonstratio liturgica*, or at least as a significant part of the *demonstratio catholica*. If so, then how should liturgy be included in theology's reflections on its sources and their authority, and on method?

In an attempt to save fundamental theologians from the embarrassment of liturgy-forgetfulness, some might answer that wherever in fundamental theology it reads "history" or "church," one may also read "liturgy." The downside to this is that liturgy becomes little more than a variety of any form of human action, at best a symbolic representation of the idea of salvation, a rituality of some sorts. Rituals and symbols, however, could never stand the test of being a theological source or foundation, and if they would be identified as one of the *loci theologici*, then probably as one of the non-proper theological ones, among other *loci* of modern theology, like "world" or "human existence." These

7. Guy Mansini, OSB, *Fundamental Theology* (Washington, DC: Catholic University of America Press, 2018).

sources are encompassing, but therefore also quite diffuse, all too general descriptions of situations and contexts, while liturgy, on the contrary, should first and foremost signify a specific *form* rather than a general *situation*, a real *presence* rather than an *interpretation*, the *theological* rather than the *existential*, in other words: the *sacramental* rather than the *ritual*. So, in order to avoid this pitfall of putting the liturgy under the general heading of history or ritual, it is necessary to reflect on the proper—revelatory and salvific—place of liturgy and sacraments in fundamental theology.

Contrary to fundamental theology, the field of liturgical theology has paid attention to the liturgy as a foundation of faith and to the relationship between liturgy and revelation. Most explicitly, this has been done by Jeremy Driscoll, who wrote in his *Theology at the Eucharistic Table*: "what I want to do here is draw the attention of liturgists to Fundamental Theology and of fundamental theologians to Liturgical Theology."[8] That call for a mutual interest between the fields was taken up by Laurence Paul Hemming, who claimed in his book *Worship as a Revelation* that "liturgy, and the study of the meaning of the liturgical texts, is the inner unity and very possibility of every other subject in the theological curriculum."[9] Hemming acknowledges that the liturgical is intrinsic to the whole of theology, and therefore foundational to theological method. In his *Thinking Prayer*, Andrew Prevot states similarly that, following the principle of *lex orandi, lex credendi*, "as a general rule, it seems appropriate to treat liturgy as the first and last theology and as theology's most definitive source."[10] This has also clearly been the mission of David Fagerberg in most of his works, initially in *Theology Prima*, one of the best contemporary examples of liturgical theology as fundamental theology.[11]

8. Jeremy Driscoll, *Theology at the Eucharistic Table* (Leonminster: Gracewing, 2003), 100.

9. Laurence Paul Hemming, *Worship as a Revelation: The Past, Present and Future of Catholic Liturgy* (London: Burns & Oates, 2008), 45.

10. Andrew Prevot, *Thinking Prayer: Theology and Spirituality amid the Crisis of Modernity* (Notre Dame, IN: University of Notre Dame Press, 2015), 29.

11. David Fagerberg, *Theologia Prima: What Is Liturgical Theology?* (Chicago: Hillenbrand Books, 2004); Fagerberg, *Liturgical Dogmatics: How Catholic Beliefs Flow from Liturgical Prayer* (San Francisco: Ignatius Press, 2021).

Philip Caldwell has published an impressive overview of the twentieth-century developments toward a foundational liturgical theology.[12] Interestingly, he starts the history of these developments with Leo XIII, whose papacy is often seen as the start of the church's attention to social and political issues.[13] Caldwell shows that since then, the relationship between liturgy and revelation has received ample attention from theologians, especially since the parallel rise of the Liturgical Movement and *ressourcement* theology, on which Chenu builds his liturgical ideas. But Caldwell also shows that the major thinkers who have renewed the idea of liturgy as revelation have been inspired by Henri de Lubac and not least by Chenu, most notably Gustave Martelet, SJ, who developed a sacramental anthropology.[14]

Contextualizing Chenu's Theology of the Liturgy: Influences and Sources

The work of Marie-Dominique Chenu would not be the obvious starting point for a reflection on either fundamental theology or liturgy, let alone on their relationship. Chenu never wrote an extensive fundamental theology, although his *Une école de théologie* could be regarded as a concise one. In it, however, he offered only a brief systematic treatment of faith and history, and of theological method, and he chose an historical approach when he discussed the relationship of philosophy and theology.[15] The articles on liturgy he wrote throughout his career, and which are translated for publication in this volume, mainly focus on anthropology rather than on faith and revelation. Therefore, some reconstruction of his work in this respect is needed.

12. Philip Caldwell, *Liturgy as Revelation: Re-Sourcing a Theme in Twentieth-Century Catholic Theology*, Renewal: Conversations in Catholic Theology (Minneapolis: Fortress Press, 2014).

13. Stephan van Erp, "World and Sacrament: Foundations of the Political Theology of the Church," *Louvain Studies* 39, no. 2 (2016): 102–20.

14. van Erp, "World and Sacrament," 337–402.

15. Marie-Dominique Chenu, *Une école de théologie: le Saulchoir* (Paris: Cerf, 1985). ET: *A School of Theology: Le Saulchoir*, trans. and ed. Joseph A. Komonchak and Mary Kate Holman (Adelaide: ATF Press, 2023).

Despite the fact that Chenu's material is limited, there are ways of finding resources in his work for a reflection on the place of liturgy in fundamental theology. I propose starting with the following texts: his views on the distinction between contemplation and speculation in his dissertation *De Contemplatione*;[16] the place of liturgy and sacraments in his thoughts on the nature of the study of theology in *Une école de théologie*, although this requires some extrapolations from his ideas in it on the religious life, Dominican spirituality, and sacramental theology in medieval studies; the role of the liturgy in *La Theologie est-elle une science?*, an essay on theology, faith, and method;[17] and his contribution to *Optatam Totius*, about which Josepf Fuchs, SJ, wrote: "the decree on the formation of priests at the very least indirectly rehabilitates Chenu."[18]

It would be in the spirit of Chenu's own theology to contextualize these documents, and it is crucial to understand his thoughts on liturgy as the result of, or better still, as the response to a complex of factors, to wit: the variety of twentieth-century Thomisms;[19] his vision for Le Saulchoir and the "Chenu affair" that followed after;[20] his "membership" of the *ressourcement* theologians; his engagement with the worker-priests; the consequences of *Humani Generis*; and his contribution to Vatican II, especially to *Optatam Totius*. I do not have much to add to the contextualizing work that Mary Kate Holman has already done in her contribution to this volume.

For the relation between liturgy and fundamental theology, however, one should not underestimate the thematic and methodological starting

16. Recently translated from Latin into French: Marie-Dominique Chenu, "'De Contemplatione': Thèse de doctorat, Angelicum, 1920," *Revue des sciences philosophiques et théologiques* 105, no. 4 (2021): 537–676.

17. Marie-Dominique Chenu, *La Théologie est-elle une science* (Paris: Librairie Arthème Fayard, 1957). ET: *Is Theology a Science?* (New York: Hawthorn Books, 1959).

18. Grant Kaplan, "The Renewal of Ecclesiastical Studies: Chenu, Tübingen, and Theological Method in *Optatam Totius*," *Theological Studies* 77 (2016): 567–92, here 592.

19. Fergus Kerr, *After Aquinas: Versions of Thomism* (Malden, MA: Blackwell, 2002), 55–56.

20. For the Chenu Affair, see Étienne Fouilloux, "L'affaire Chenu: 1937–1943," *Revue des sciences philosophiques et théologiques* 98 (2014): 261–352.

point of the young Chenu—contemplation and spirituality—as an important source for understanding his theology. Despite their differences, one should pay attention to the influence of Réginald Garrigou-Legrange, Chenu's doctoral supervisor, and Ambroise Gardeil, his student master at Le Saulchoir. Dominican spirituality flourished in the early decades of the twentieth century, especially in French- and Spanish-speaking theology. It coincided with the ascent of Leonine Thomism in the years of recovery from the quietist crisis, which also saw a growing influence of Carmelite voices in Catholic spirituality, with a special interest in the nature of contemplation. The era's most influential Dominican theologian, especially on the spiritual life, was Réginald Garrigou-Lagrange, who has been recently nicknamed "the sacred monster of Thomism."[21] Not only did he supervise Chenu's doctoral thesis on contemplation, but he also published his books on the spiritual life, *Christian Perfection and Contemplation* (1923) and *The Three Ages of the Interior Life* (1938), which both articulated a doctrinal synthesis of spiritual progress and contemplation.[22] This synthesis proved to be formative for Chenu's position on the liturgy.

In the same period, Gardeil completed a dense two-volume work of speculative mystical theology, entitled *La structure de l'âme et l'expérience mystique*, which would in fact be the last book he published during his lifetime.[23] This work by his former student master at Le Saulchoir disappointed Garrigou-Lagrange, who sharply critiqued its main thesis, the possibility of a direct experience of God in this life through mystical experience.[24] This debate concerned burning ques-

21. Richard Peddicourt, *The Sacred Monster of Thomism: An Introduction to the Life and Legacy of Réginald Garrigou-Lagrange OP* (South Bend, IN: St. Augustine's Press, 2005).

22. Réginald Garrigou-Lagrange, *Perfection chrétienne et contemplation selon S. Thomas d'Aquin et S. Jean de la Croix*, 2 vols. (Saint-Maximin: Editions de la Vie spirituelle, 1923); Garrigou-Lagrange, *Christian Perfection and Contemplation according to St. Thomas Aquinas and St. John of the Cross*, trans. M. Timothea Doyle (London: Herder, 1937); Garrigou-Lagrange, *Les trois âges de la vie intérieure: prélude de celle du ciel*, 3 vols. (Paris: Cerf, 1938); Garrigou-Lagrange, *The Three Ages of the Interior Life: Prelude to Eternal Life*, 2 vols. (London: Herder, 1947–48).

23. Ambroise Gardeil, *La structure de l'âme et l'expérience mystique*, 2 vols. (Paris: Librairie Victor Lecoffre, 1927).

24. Réginald Garrigou-Lagrange, "L'habitation de la sainte Trinité et l'expérience mystique," *La Revue Thomiste* 33 (1928): 449–78.

tions that formed the background of Chenu's years as a teacher at Le Saulchoir, including the function of concepts in spirituality and prayer, the distinction between the praying subject and the divine object, and more broadly, the types of theological arguments that have been employed in developing a modern theology of spirituality. For that reason, we need a better historical hermeneutic of these influences—not only of Gardeil and Garrigou-Lagrange, but also of the emerging theologies of spirituality of that period—of the *ressourcement* theologians, crucial for understanding contemporary theology; and of Chenu in our particular case, in order to better understand the gradual formation of theological schools and movements, and their mutual relations up to the council's documents on priestly formation and the religious life. Furthermore, this historical hermeneutic will show clear parallels with the development of the Liturgical Movement, and of modern liturgical theology in its wake.

Reconstructing Chenu's Theology of Liturgy: Truth Resides in Mystery

In the 1930s, Chenu had become convinced that theology should reflect on the contemporary human situation and God's involvement in it. According to him, faith and theology do not so much build on an unchanging depositum of revelation that God has placed in the hands of the church, which has preserved it through the centuries, but on God's dynamic presence in human history. This was in line with his historical reading of Aquinas's premise that theology is the study of God and of everything *sub ratione Dei* with significant consequences for his view on theological method: theological sources and doctrines must be understood as part of a living, historically developing faith. To Chenu, Christian history is a living reality, and not a fixed set of formal propositions. Such claims can become empty slogans, and in contemporary theology, they certainly have. Yet, according to Grant Kaplan, in Chenu's theology these claims carry with them "a methodological imperative to investigate historical epochs as ongoing manifestations of the salvation-historical events recorded in Scripture."[25] History and the development of ideas, however, demand rational justification. Despite

25. Cf. Kaplan, "The Renewal of Ecclesiastical Studies," 582.

Chenu's historical approach of Aquinas's thought, he did appreciate scholasticism and its rational method for turning theology into a science. Therefore, he believes theology's method needs to be scriptural, historical, and experiential, but its aim is intellectual and theoretical.

What does this mean for his view on liturgy as a foundation for theology? Probably not that the liturgy provides the experiences for which theology then provides the rational structures: liturgy as the practice on which theological theory is built. In the 1947 article "Anthropology and Liturgy," he writes that liturgy is nourished by divine tradition *and* human traditions, and that it is both revelational *and* historical, theological *and* anthropological.[26] To Chenu, liturgy is therefore in and of itself revelational and theological, which means that theology does not merely provide or unpack the meaning and interpretation of liturgy, but that liturgy itself provides theological content. In the spirit of *ressourcement*, he argues that theological method does not relate to liturgy as theory relates to practice, or as content relates to form, but, as he writes in the same article, as truth that resides *in* liturgy: liturgy is intrinsically shaped and informed by theology and thus shapes and informs theology.[27] It is the catholic "in" in the original meaning of *kata* in the word *katholou* (meaning "in or through the whole") that raises the question whether this dwelling is merely a form of mediation or accommodation, or the objective dynamic of revelation in liturgy itself. Chenu seems to affirm the latter when he writes about the objective content of the liturgy, and about the incarnation as its prototype.

This is why Chenu's theology could help us understand liturgy not merely as a home or an expression of theology, but as theology proper; not just as a *locus* that demands theological interpretation, but as a revelatory, and therefore theologically authoritative, source in itself. Elsewhere, he writes: "The liturgy, the mysterious presence of God through the intermediary of symbols, is the vital environment in which the primitive religious powers of human beings find their balance." And he continues: "It is also, in the positive revelation of Christ, the vital environment in which faith can develop rationally, without reducing

26. Chenu 1947, par. 1, 2.
27. Chenu 1947, par. 4.

the irrational elements of its 'initiation.'"[28] So, both symbolic mediation and the rationality of faith are grounded in liturgy, which in turn is qualified by the mystery of God's presence and by the positive revelation of Christ. This, in a nutshell, is liturgy as fundamental theology.

Apart from these formal theological principles, Chenu also had historical, situational reasons to hold a plea for liturgy as theology, when he used it as a correction of both the naturalism *and* the anti-intellectualism of his time. In a style that immediately shows his closeness to the *ressourcement* theologians, and one that nowadays perhaps could be identified as Radical Orthodoxy's, he writes: "the primary trait of the new humanity that we see born in this twentieth century, in extravagant outbursts, is the violent growth of these irrational elements, either supra or infra-rational."[29] On the one hand, Chenu warns against the dangerous anti-intellectualism and its political and social consequences in his time, in an article written just after the Second World War. On the other hand, he appreciates a long-term cultural and philosophical response against modern rationalism, and what he calls the "natural theology" of the eighteenth century, which relegated the symbolic and the mystical to the margins of the sacred. He, however, advocates a liturgical, and not merely a moral, correction of the situation in the church, because liturgy could provide a renewed balance between the symbolic and the real, and between the mystical and the rational.

Chenu writes perhaps most explicitly about the revelatory dimensions of the liturgy in his book *La Theologie est-elle une science?* Against the idea of identifying theology with catechesis, he argues for a theology that is rooted in the divine mystery realized in the sacraments, and he praises Pius XII's liturgical revival of the Easter Vigil, which according to him has rightly fostered a more lucid theology of the resurrection, for, as he writes, "theology is the science of salvation. One enters it by an 'initiation,' and for this the liturgy provides both the ritual and the light. Once again we see that theology remains within the mystery."[30] For Chenu, the study of liturgy is a "science" in a particular way, which

28. Chenu 1947, par. 18.
29. Chenu 1947, par. 7.
30. Chenu, *Is Theology a Science?*, 46.

should not so much limit itself to the definition and enumeration of the seven sacraments, "leaving the practice of them to be controlled by those who administer them, the liturgiologists or the casuists."[31] On the contrary, he acknowledges that the liturgical revival of his time gained its power from sources far beyond mere pastoral or aesthetic concerns. He sees it as the result of a new theological appreciation for the mystery of Christ, as a source that undergirds both liturgical and theological developments, with both formal and doctrinal consequences, which should be treated together, rather than separately. "The theologian regards the liturgy as the special sanctuary of the faith, where the Church proclaims her message even while she prays."[32]

In his later articles on the liturgy, Chenu concentrates on anthropological aspects. Interestingly, he uses the connatural communication between the divine and the human spirit as a marker for the distinction between worship that is rooted in the incarnation, and any other form of religious worship.[33] In his article on sacramental anthropology, he grounds humanity in the sacramentality of the cosmos.[34] What could be perceived as a postconciliar anthropological turn in Chenu's theology is in fact a more Christocentric and metaphysical—ontological, material—grounding of liturgy. Unfortunately, liturgy has become the battlefield where the polarization in the church only seems to increase. A renewed reading of Chenu's liturgical approach, despite its anthropological overtones, might contribute to a better mutual understanding between the so-called "traditional" and "liberal" positions, precisely because he connects the sacramental and the social in a new, incarnational way, which could appeal to both camps.

Conclusion: *Mysterium Fidei*

Chenu's theology of liturgy could, apart from helping us to understand the liturgy as revelation, also be useful as a correction of an all too epistemological and rationalist understanding of the task of

31. Chenu, *Is Theology a Science?*, 60.
32. Chenu, *Is Theology a Science?*, 61.
33. Chenu 1967, par. 6–7.
34. Chenu 1974, par. 24.

fundamental theology. At the same time, he argued against a mere symbolic or mystical understanding of liturgy, and for that reason advocated a theology that was grounded in the liturgical. The history of theology, he writes, "is full of such symbolic elaborations, within the fabric of the revelation itself. The Fathers, both in their sermons and in their writings, continually nourish their *intellectus fidei* with such symbolism."[35] There is an opportunity here for fundamental theology to integrate liturgy as *mysterium fidei*, besides, or perhaps even as an initiation to and foundation of the *auditus* and *intellectus fidei*.

In *Optatam Totius*—a document on which Chenu has had a profound influence, even though he was disappointed by the end result—the council fathers call for theology to be renewed through a more vivid contact with the mystery of Christ and the history of salvation.[36] The history of theology, the document states, does not solely depend on the development of its dogmas, but also on its lived, incarnated practices and liturgical forms, which are appreciated precisely because they lend, perhaps paradoxically, greater intelligibility to the form of revelation. Here, we encounter liturgy as the motif for the development of the history of theology. It should be a call to fundamental theologians to explicitly include the liturgical in their rational account of the sources and method of theology.

35. Chenu, *Is Theology a Science?*, 85.

36. *Optatam Totius*, Decree on Priestly Training, proclaimed by Pope Paul VI on October 28, 1965, no. 16.

Contemporary Challenges for Sacramental Theology

Joris Geldhof

In the introduction to his noted volume *The Sacraments*, Kevin Irwin defines sacramental theology as "the systematic study of the sacraments based on a prayerful reflection of the liturgical celebration of these rites throughout history, and on the insights of theologians and other teachers in light of the church's magisterium."[1] This definition has at least three advantages: (i) unlike many attempts from the past, it includes liturgy as an evident source and resource for theological thinking and scientific research on the sacraments; (ii) it embraces a historical approach in view of systematic reflection and thereby considers tradition as something dynamic; and (iii) it suggests that one can find and do sacramental theology beyond the confines of ecclesial teaching and the writings of the usual suspects in the canon of classical sacramental theology (but not fundamentally opposed to what these authorities have said). However, Irwin's definition also has a major shortcoming, in that it actually only refers to "the sacraments" and not to the broader phenomenon of sacramentality.

For the reflections below I understand sacramental theology as the art of understanding and explaining God's saving proximity to humanity, in particular in and through the liturgical celebrations in remembrance of

1. Kevin W. Irwin, *The Sacraments: Historical Foundations and Liturgical Theology* (Mahwah, NJ: Paulist Press, 2016), 11–12.

the paschal mystery and everything that it encompasses and manifests. In other words, sacramental theology is not primarily a specific discipline or area of scholarship dealing with a particular topic, such as, for example, the seven sacraments which the Roman Catholic Church has recognized for ten centuries or more—as Irwin seems to imply. Rather, it is a way of doing theology, it is *doing theology sacramentally*. Thus, the adjective "sacramental" in "sacramental theology" does neither delineate an object next to other (possible) objects, nor does it indicate a precise method for approaching the object, but it determines and qualifies (a) theology as such. The "sacramental" nature of theology refers to the mystery of God's salvific plan for humankind, its definitive revelation in the Christ event, the many manifestations of that in history, and the multivalent mediations of all of that through established rituals, rhythms of praying, prayers themselves, cultural expressions, social traditions, human experiences, and works of art.

Consequently, an argument could be set up that any theology ought to be (ultimately, at least inchoately) sacramental, because theologians cannot avoid the question of how God is (sacramentally) present and involved in the world, in history, in human lives and interactions, and in the church. If the labor of theologians does not somehow contribute to better understanding and explaining *how* that is the case, what are their theologies then *for*? However, that argument is not at stake here. Instead I intend to specify with the aid of Chenu's creative thinking on the matter what it means that sacraments and sacramentality impact theology as a whole, that is, they set an *agenda* for contemporary theology—literally, in the sense of ordering what has to be done. Theology done sacramentally today means that theologians actively seek ways (methods, illustrations, sources, examples, texts, artistic expressions, objects, music, experiences, testimonies, etc.) which point in the direction of what God, at least according to the Scriptures and the Christian tradition, has always done and presumably continues to do, namely to *be there* for humans in a way that is *good* for them. In other words, sacramental theology aims at understanding the particularities and details of the history of salvation as well as the underlying mechanism of the economy of salvation.[2]

2. To further elaborate on this point, inspiration can be drawn from an absolute classic in liturgical theology: Cipriano Vagaggini, *Theological Dimensions of the Liturgy: A General Treatise on the Theology of Liturgy* (Collegeville, MN: Liturgical Press, 1976).

The hypothesis undergirding the present reflections is that Chenu's explorations at the intersection of anthropology, theology, and liturgy are instrumental in this respect. It is supposed that Chenu helps us understand how theology today can be done in a sacramental mode. In view of demonstrating how that is the case I will proceed in four steps; in so doing, four different challenges for contemporary sacramental theologians will be discerned and discussed. First, I propose a reconsideration of sacramentality as something actively at work rather than a static situation. Second, in line with Pope Francis's recent document on liturgical formation *Desiderio Desideravi*,[3] I would like to tackle the fundamental problem of modern and postmodern people's capacity for liturgy or, in the vocabulary famously employed by Romano Guardini, *Liturgiefähigkeit*. I would like to reformulate the issue at stake in terms of a fundamental human incapacity for sacraments and sacramentality, *Sakramentenunfähigkeit*. Third, I will address the problem of sacramental realism from the angle of human solidarity. What binds human beings beyond the boundaries of their own attempts at ordering the lifeworld in accordance with their insights and faculties is a sacramental reality of sorts. Finally, I will wrap up the preceding reflections and offer some thoughts about the perpetually urgent problem of the pertinence of Christian sacraments.

God's Saving Presence in Time

It is striking how many times and how strongly Chenu insists that the Christian sacramental system is something actively at work. Sacramentality is not a situation; it is an operation. It is the perpetuation of the economy of salvation,[4] the origins of which are to be situated in God's unreserved and unfailing love of humankind, in other words, in God's revelation itself and the corresponding universal salvific plan. The primary means of communicating this plan are deeds, whereby one needs to realize that, according to an ancient Semitic understanding, words also are deeds (*dabar*). Words, particularly words of God, and thus also sacramental words, *do* something—as can be

3. https://www.vatican.va/content/francesco/en/apost_letters/documents/20220629-lettera-ap-desiderio-desideravi.html.

4. Chenu 1952, par. 1–10; 1962, par. 20; 1974, par. 2.

powerfully shown through an analysis of Liturgies of the Word and the Paschal Vigil very specifically.[5] They perform, bring about, shape, establish, institute, constitute, inspire, incite, ignite, etc. Nothing less than God's agency is to be suspected behind its many manifestations and expressions. That implies that what it accomplishes is often invisible and to a certain extent also incomprehensible for human beings.

The being-at-work of sacramentality challenges classical patterns of thinking, even if, as Chenu rightly indicates, they have been and still are accurate.[6] According to Chenu, as well as to his pupil Schillebeeckx, there is a great amount of continuity between the deepest sacramental theological intuitions of the church fathers and those of the great medieval master theologians; there is a core of sacramental doctrine which is true independent of always contingent conceptualizations of it.[7] A pertinent question, then, is to what extent these thought patterns are still helpful, and whether they aptly catch the actual concerns and match with the ways of thinking and living of people today. There is ample reason for doubt here, and certainly for caution.

One way to try to make sense of the operativity of sacramentality is putting forward the idea that a (more) *verbal* understanding of the concept-and-reality of sacramentality would be welcome. This verbal understanding would contrast with an understanding of sacramentality as a noun. Of course, from a grammatical point of view, in En-

5. Irwin, *The Sacraments*, 254–72; 287–92. That said, it is a pity that Chenu himself, unlike Irwin, hardly gives, let alone elaborates upon, concrete textual examples taken from liturgical books.

6. This would, for example, apply to the way of presenting fundamental thoughts on the sacraments through the vocabulary of Aristotelian hylemorphism (circling around the concepts of matter and form) and its philosophical presuppositions. On the one hand, this schema is no longer pertinent to encompass the complexity of what is being talked about. On the other hand, one cannot deny that a deep truth lies in this to some extent idiosyncratic conceptualization: in order for there to be a sacrament, crucial words (from Scripture) are to be somehow combined with materiality and corporeality (significant gestures).

7. Edward Schillebeeckx, *De sacramentele heilseconomie: Theologische bezinning op S. Thomas' sacramentenleer in het licht van de traditie en van de hedendaagse sacramentsproblematiek* (Antwerp: 't Groeit–H. Nelissen, 1952), 387. It should be reiterated here that Schillebeeckx was a student of Chenu during his formation years at Le Saulchoir.

glish as in many other Indo-European languages, sacramentality is a noun and not a verb.[8] The point is that this very linguistic structure determines the ways in which sacramentality is conceived of, associated with, imagined, spoken of, thought about, reflected upon, etc. What would be the effects if sacramentality were not a noun but a verb? The whole syntax and semantics of it would change. And maybe that would come closer to what sacramentality "is" and what it "does." As it now stands, the word "sacramentality" works within the same framework of a logic of attribution which impacts so much of our thinking, perceiving, and organizing of the lifeworld. It means that we naturally connect sacramentality with adjectives and say things about it as if it were a thing indeed. Yet sacramentality is not a thing, certainly not a graspable one, not a substance, not an object, to which characteristics (rightly or wrongly) can be attributed. Sacramentality is fundamentally verbal and is more appropriately approached by adverbs further refining how it works, when it works, where it works, why it works, for what and whom it works, etc.

It follows from the above that sacraments are first and foremost actions or events (with actions), but certainly not things or objects—long before Louis-Marie Chauvet, Chenu showed himself a fierce opponent to any sacramental "*chosification*."[9] This is a unique French term by which is understood the turning of something into an object or a thing (*une chose*), a reification or solidification as it were, eliminating its dynamic. Sacraments are particular instances of the broader sacramental operativity of the economy of salvation. They embody and express sacramentality, actively, verbally. They escape the grip of the

8. By way of parallel, consider those languages—including Hopi, Navajo, and some languages spoken by First Nations in Australia—in which the concepts of a "fire" and "flames" are not expressed through a noun but through a verb. This changes a lot, not only practically at the level of the culture but also in the world of thinking and the imagination. Cf. the groundbreaking work of George Lakoff and Mark Johnson in the field of cognitive linguistics (in particular, their influential book *Metaphors We Live By* from 1980).

9. Louis-Marie Chauvet, *Symbol and Sacrament: A Sacramental Reinterpretation of Christian Existence* (Collegeville, MN: Liturgical Press, 1995). Together with Schillebeeckx (and Rahner), Chauvet is often considered one of the most important innovators of (Roman Catholic) sacramental theology in the twentieth century.

logic of attribution and qualify reality itself. They are not add-ons, but inextricably interwoven with the fabric of reality, and with life itself. The specificity of the sacraments, moreover, consists in their being *symbolic* actions. Again, long before Chauvet, Chenu examines the intrinsic connection between symbol and sacrament, or symbol and mystery.[10] Both of them are actions and ontologically prior to any conceptualization. They are more deeply rooted in the human condition than the capacity for thinking rationally. They mean by doing; therefore, their meaning is not added to but precisely in their being accomplished. They do not avoid matter but literally go through it. Chenu has a lot of attention for this basic level of sheer materiality, again in line with much of what the church fathers already taught, sometimes in polemical contexts against Manichaean and other dualistic worldviews,[11] which actually looked down upon matter and the body.

It is important not only to observe the active nature of sacraments and sacramentality but also to ask what it is that they do. In a way, they are the engine of the transformation of world and history which is the result of God's salvific will (as expressing God's ceaseless love of humankind). This transformation is far from accomplished but Christians believe it is in the process of realizing itself. Its connection with time and history is not extrinsic but intrinsic, and the sacraments establish a natural bond with the past, the present, and the future simultaneously.[12] The arch-model for this transformation of "being and time" is the paschal mystery, as exemplified by Jesus' transition from death to life, from suffering to joy, and from indifference to love.

The appropriate response to all of this from the side of human beings is certainly not some kind of passivity, as corresponding to sacramentality's and the individual sacraments' activity. Rather, it is a porous

10. As a matter of fact, Chenu comes back to that connection in all the articles presented in this book; see Chenu 1947, par. 14; 1952, par. 18; 1962, par. 14; 1967, par. 32–37; 1974, par. 29. Thus, it is fair to say that this connection is the focal point of Chenu's sacramental theology and a major contribution to thinking in that area.

11. A fitting example here could be Tertullian's defense of the use of water in baptism (cf. Irwin, *The Sacraments*, 45–46).

12. Chenu alludes to Thomas Aquinas where the Angelic Doctor says that the sacramental signs are commemorative, indicative, and prognostic, thereby encompassing the three dimensions of time (past, present, future). See Chenu 1952, par. 26.

receptivity, expressing itself as a willingness and readiness to cooperate with the grand transformation in the name and by virtue of God's love. The sacraments create a system to step into this encompassing transformative dynamic, which is possible at any time and at any place.

The Problem of *Sakramentenunfähigkeit*

The problem of the human being's capacity for liturgy has been a preoccupation of many theologians belonging to the Liturgical Movement. Since its inception there have been discussions about the alienating effects of a rapidly developing industrial culture on humans' "natural" bonds, not only with nature but also with each other and with God.[13] As a matter of fact, the evolution of modern culture was not infrequently looked upon with a large amount of suspicion, even if later representatives of the movement wholeheartedly embraced a certain form of belief in humankind's progress; they were at least optimistic about the efficacy of organized programs to bring about change. Interestingly, Romano Guardini's dealings with the human being's *Liturgiefähigkeit*, or rather the lack of it, can be read as a sparkle of skepticism in the midst of these evolutions.

Guardini seems to associate *Liturgiefähigkeit* with the capacity for symbols. He assumes that symbols are fragile and vulnerable when confronted with rationalistic, scientific, and analytic approaches to reality. The more reason dictates human interaction with the world, the less symbols can manifest themselves and impact human thought and experience. In other words, according to Guardini, as well as to Pope Francis, a preservation of symbols and the general human sensitivity for symbolicity regardless of all kinds of rationalizations of the lifeworld is a prerequisite for the liturgy to have a future and a real meaning, both for individual people and communities.[14] While there is certainly truth in these assumptions, there is also a risk involved in

13. In this context, there are striking parallels between Odo Casel and Martin Heidegger; both of them give evidence of a fundamental mistrust towards "technology" and, indeed, sometimes a rather pessimistic worldview.

14. Cf. *Desiderio Desideravi* 44, with a reference to his 1923 essay *Liturgische Bildung*.

the reduction of (Christian) liturgy to (human and always material) symbols. Put differently, even if human beings remain prone to symbols and the way they work (upon them), it is not a given that liturgy will persist.

This observation raises the question at which level the assertion that human beings (increasingly) lack *Liturgiefähigkeit* has to be situated. Is it merely a matter of cultural criticism, and therefore necessarily contextual? Is it an anthropological contention, implying something about the very nature of being human? Or is it an ontological claim, or a theological conviction? At this point enters Chenu.

Chenu certainly shares the observation that it is neither evident nor easy to involve modern people in a symbolic network, especially not in a narrative symbolically mediating the Christian faith. There is a lot of reluctance among people to continue to engage in liturgical and other symbolic practices. Yet, without any symbolicity, human existence seems to lose something essential, even if it is difficult to indicate with exactitude what that essential something would be.[15] This suggests that for Chenu the sensitivity for symbols is an anthropological given, even an important or a crucial one. At the same time, it is a theological idea, inasmuch as the human talent for symbols constitutes the ground receptivity for God's work of salvation.

However, this talent not only often fails, it fails structurally, in the sense that it can never achieve perfection. The human being never gets out of themself enough to be an ideal or complete receptacle of God's love, grace, and redemption. For this reason, which has to do with the fundamental asymmetry between God and humankind, one can speak of a deep-rooted *Sakramentenunfähigkeit* in the human condition. A lack of *Liturgiefähigkeit*, dependent on contingent sociocultural, spiritual, and intellectual factors, can never compensate for *Sakramentenunfähigkeit*. And conversely, a *Liturgiefähigkeit* bordering on perfec-

15. It is probably the human capacity for language that comes into purview here, something that Chenu alludes to but which he does not really elaborate in depth in the texts under consideration. One could argue that someone like Chauvet took up that thread (cf. footnote 9). In any case, there is a remarkable correspondence between these two thinkers with respect to the case they make for taking up insights from the humanities into sacramental theology. See Chenu 1974, par. 6.

tion also does not automatically generate a *Sakramentenfähigkeit*. The best humanly possible liturgy is never a guarantee of dignity to receive sacramental grace. Chenu is disarmingly levelheaded about this.

Sacramentality at the Roots of Solidarity

Chenu defends a firm realism in sacramental theology. The roots of it lie in the theological tradition, which he obviously knew very well. Unsurprisingly, Chenu regularly refers to Thomas Aquinas as a major source of inspiration, not only to provide evidence of that realism in the past but also in view of contributing to contemporary sacramental theological questions.[16] For Chenu, Aquinas's sacramental theology is exemplary in that it understands how to match the mysteries of faith with the reality of (human) life. In so doing it sets a model for any other theological attempt at making sense of Christian sacramentality.

What is striking is that Chenu insists on this realism without emphasizing too much on related categories such as objectivity, validity, and institution. There is no doubt that the sacraments have been instituted, that there have to be rules for their official recognition and transmission, and that there is something to them beyond mere convention and habits. Chenu does not deny the importance of any of these ideas, yet he does not buy into a classical sacramental objectivism. On the other hand, Chenu does not advocate subjectivism in sacramental theology either, since the basis of the sacraments is to a certain extent independent from feelings, impressions, personal memories, and the successes of human-made organizations. Chenu just avoids any risk of being caught in a simple yes-or-no game between subjectivists and objectivists in sacramental theory.[17] More important than rooting sacramental realism in conflicting ontologies or epistemologies is realizing the soteriological, doxological, and eschatological reality

16. Chenu 1952, par. 30–31; 1974, par. 3.

17. In this respect also, Chenu anticipates a lot of what Chauvet has later developed in a lot more detail. The attention for the indispensability of (multiple material) mediations, accessible for the human senses, is a crucial point that today is taken for granted by any sacramental theologian.

which, establishing the sacramental principle of Christianity and thus its entire sacramentality, grounds every sacrament and sacramental.

There is one particular aspect or dimension of this grand sacramental reality that I hold particularly important today, because it is often threatened or neglected. One could call it an ecclesiological dimension, since it concerns the church (and its synodal and missionary nature). But one could—and maybe should—equally call it an anthropological dimension, since it concerns humanity and an inclusive concept of personhood in particular, which the Christian religion is bound to develop and defend, at least if it wants to stay faithful to its founding event, the paschal mystery, including the incarnation. Chenu helps us understand better how the ecclesiological and the anthropological interact,[18] and how they should always interact, especially in a climate where the church seems increasingly dissociated from people and from what is human (in spite of Pope Francis, who, intriguingly, seems on Chenu's side in this respect), and where what is said about being human is frequently disconnected from the church and the role it ought to play in the sublunary.

A strong realistic sacramental vision seems crucial both for the (future of the) church and for a global and truly inclusive humanity. The universal salvation of humankind is neither a dry objective fact or principle, nor the result of subjective opinions or debates about them. It is an engaging and enthusing reality of infinite proportions, into which the Christian sacraments relentlessly invite and initiate, and which they also uniquely give shape to. Ultimately, Christian sacramentality is all about sharing the Body and Blood of Christ, in which is symbolically embodied the fullness of the mysteries, and there is never a reason not to put forth an effort to involve everybody in that.

In other words, Christian sacraments and sacramentality mediate a universal reality which they neither own nor have invented. They establish a unity "in Christ," the boundaries of which exceed beyond the limits of time and space. For the community worshiping "with Him, through Him and in Him" includes past generations, angels, saints, and the deceased, as well as future generations, known and unknown. In this universalism, which is not ideological, political, or historical

18. Chenu 1962, par. 8 (intriguingly, Chenu quotes Schillebeeckx here); 1967, par. 21–23, 42.

but "simply" sacramental, and therefore real, lie the deepest roots for interhuman solidarity—a kind of solidarity that can never result out of a common set of ideas, values, organizations, or realizations.[19] I think it is a kind of unity and solidarity that the world urgently needs. It is a kind of solidarity that does not depend on who or what people are or what they think they are or have to be, but instead is rooted in the fact *that* they are (loved by God).

Concluding Observations

In conclusion, it is fair to say that Chenu is a great help and a true source of inspiration for doing theology sacramentally today. According to him, the sacraments are rooted in sacramentality, and sacramentality is not just an added layer of meaning, which one can accept or reject on a purely subjective basis. Put differently, sacramentality is not alien to reality as it is. Therefore, unlike several (sometimes fashionable and popular) tendencies in fundamental and systematic theology today, Chenu decidedly holds on to a strong metaphysical claim at the heart of sacramental theology. Like Schillebeeckx and even Chauvet after him, he can be considered a keen defender of a non-extrinsicist position: sacraments and sacramentality are not extrinsic to being, but intrinsically interwoven with the way in which reality is accessible for human beings. The key to that access is the potential of symbols for signification. These processes of signification happen primarily not through rational communication and explication but through the body and the senses—whence the fascinating concept of a sacramental/symbolic/mystery-bearing "density," to which Chenu time and again refers. Maybe it is in the explorations of how this density works that Chenu's greatest gift for a sacramental theology today is lying.

Yet, even if Chenu is not a frequent reference in contemporary sacramental theology,[20] it is worth reading and rereading his essays on

19. For a further elaboration of this point, see also my programmatic article "Pour un nouvel universalisme liturgique," in *La Maison-Dieu* 308 (2022): 135–54.

20. There is not a single mention of him in two recent compendia: Hans Boersma and Matthew Levering, eds., *The Oxford Handbook of Sacramental Theology* (Oxford: Oxford University Press, 2015), and Martha Moore-Keish and James W. Farwell, eds., *T&T Clark Handbook of Sacraments and Sacramentality* (London: T&T Clark, 2023).

the matter. In particular, in view of the omnipresent and multivarious life-liturgy gap, which largely corresponds with the sacraments-world gap as well as the church-society/culture gap, his texts have profound insights to offer. This is true for both the content of Chenu's thinking and his approach. What he says is often still relevant, maybe surprisingly, but not so surprisingly as one digs deeper into his writings. Inasmuch as one ventures to do that digging, one becomes familiar with the style, the sources, and the very way in which he was theologizing, which in the end is surprisingly (or unsurprisingly?) simple. Chenu carefully reads the tradition in view of contemporary questions, and when one does that with an honesty, lucidity, and transparency as the ones characteristic of his work, there is something movingly timeless to that. To get to that timeless core of sacramental theological thinking, more than to offer a correct interpretation of Chenu, was the endeavor of this paper.

An Interaction with Aquinas's Theology

Harm Goris

As a Catholic theologian starting his studies in the beginning of the twentieth century, and as a Dominican, it was impossible for Chenu to ignore the works of his confrere Thomas Aquinas. Chenu opposes the ahistorical reading of Aquinas's works by the neo-Thomism that was dominant in his time, and advocates instead a hermeneutical interpretation, characteristic of what later would be called the *nouvelle theologie.* Chenu also prefers a Greek approach to theology epitomized in the writings of Pseudo-Dionysius and his *exitus-reditus* scheme, to what he labels as the Augustinian, or Augustinist approach. In the context of a discussion on Chenu's view on the sacraments, I shall defend the thesis that the Pseudo-Dionysian framework makes Chenu less sensitive to two key elements in Aquinas's sacramentology: viz. the sacrament as sign within an epistemic context, and the sacrament as remedy for sin. Both elements bear the stamp of an Augustinian provenance.

I shall first outline the neo-Thomist background against which Chenu proposes his own methodological approach toward Aquinas's works: the "historical method." Next, I shall briefly discuss how Chenu takes Pseudo-Dionysius's neoplatonic *exitus-reditus* scheme as the metaphysical background for interpreting Aquinas. The last two sections offer a critical interpretation of two consequences of using this background in Chenu's sacramentology: the option for "symbol" over "sign" and the disregard of (original) sin.

Neo-Thomism

As of the second half of the nineteenth century, Catholic intellectuals began to promote Aquinas's thought as an alternative and remedy to so-called "modernism," labeled by Pius X as "the synthesis of all heresies."[1] The meaning of the term "modernism" is not very clear. It was used to indicate the philosophies of Descartes, Kant, Hegel, and Schleiermacher, but also the French Revolution, liberalism, socialism, or historical-critical biblical exegesis, and the influences these movements had on Catholic intellectuals. An important development in the rise of Neo-Thomism was Leo XIII's encyclical *Aeterni Patris, On the Restoration of Christian Philosophy,* published in 1879. The pope exhorts all bishops "to restore the golden wisdom of St. Thomas, and to spread it far and wide for the defense and beauty of the Catholic faith, for the good of society, and for the advantage of all the sciences."[2]

The polemic and apologetic context in which Aquinas was deployed during the late nineteenth and early twentieth centuries also determined the way his texts were interpreted. First, the philosophical parts of his works were abstracted from their theological framework. After all, Neo-Thomism was meant to combat secular ways of thinking, for which theological arguments are rather irrelevant and ineffective. This was different from how Aquinas had been presented as an authority in the sixteenth century in reaction to the Protestant Reformation. Second, Aquinas was supposed to offer a return to a universal *philosophia perennis.* Therefore, he was read independently of his thirteenth-century historical context. Aquinas was supposed to answer modern questions that had never been asked in his own times.

"Historical Method"

Already early on in his career, Chenu refused to go with a Neo-Thomist reading of Aquinas. He wrote his dissertation on the topic of *contemplatio* in Thomas Aquinas with Garrigou-Lagrange between

1. Pius X, encyclical *Pascendi Dominici Gregis,* On the Doctrine of the Modernists (1907), 39.

2. *Aeterni Patris* 31 (DH 3140).

1914 and 1920.[3] In the introduction of his thesis, he states, "If the opportunity arises, we'll also make timely use of the historical method, i.e., historically considering how the question arose."[4] The clause "if the opportunity arises" is not meant to marginalize the historical approach. This is clear from the end of the introduction:

> So it's not for the sake of antiquarianism that I've researched and quoted some rather obscure texts by theologians and philosophers of the thirteenth century; but because it is essential to understand the thought of St. Thomas in the milieu in which it was born, in which it developed, according to this or that reaction, under this or that influence.[5]

Garrigou-Lagrange, who was one of the fiercest fighters against "modernism," might not have been too happy with these remarks of his student.

The "historical approach" does not mean that Chenu, like a medievalist, only had a historical interest in Aquinas. Instead, he wants to read Aquinas's works theologically: investigating what Aquinas intended to say can help us now to better understand the truth about God. "Paradoxically," he writes, "the more I understand Aquinas in his time, the more I feel his relevance today."[6] In this way, Chenu thinks, he follows in the footsteps of Aquinas himself.[7] For both, theology is

3. The dissertation, written in Latin, was not published. Extracts appeared in Carmelo Giuseppe Conticello, "'De Contemplatione' (Angelicum, 1920): La thèse inédite de doctorat du P. M.-D. Chenu," *Revue des sciences philosophiques et théologiques* 75, no. 3 (1991): 363–422. An integral French translation was published in 2021: Marie-Dominique Chenu, "'De Contemplatione': Thèse de doctorat, Angelicum, 1920," *Revue des sciences philosophiques et théologiques* 105, no. 4 (2021): 537–676.

4. Chenu, "*De Contemplatione*," 544: "Si l'occasion s'en présente, nous ferons aussi un recours opportun à la méthode historique, c'est-à-dire en considérant historiquement la manière dont la question s'est posée."

5. Chenu, "*De Contemplatione*," 544.

6. Jacques Duquesne, *Jacques Duquesne interroge le Père Chenu: Un théologien en liberté* (Paris: Le Centurion, 1975), 49: "paradoxalement, plus je comprends saint Thomas dans son temps, plus j'en ressens aujourd'hui l'actualité."

7. See Marie-Dominique Chenu, *Toward Understanding Saint Thomas*, trans. Albert M. Landry and Dominic Hughes (Chicago: Henry Regnery, 1964), 153–55.

not a matter of defending or proving the doctrines of faith before the forum of a neutral reason or of a secular audience, as Neo-Thomism thought. Theology may have an apologetic function, but it is primarily *fides quaerens intellectum*, aimed at a further initiation into the faith.

Exitus-reditus and Pseudo-Dionysius

Later on in Chenu's career it becomes clear that the "historical approach" of Aquinas is not limited to methodology. Inspired by the idea that Christian faith itself is not based on eternal, necessary truths but on the contingency of God's economy of salvation,[8] Chenu also wants to read the content of Aquinas's works in a historical framework. He does so by proposing the neoplatonic *exitus-reditus* scheme as the underlying principle for the structure of the *Summa Theologiae*: the First Part of the *Summa* explains how all emanates from God. The Second Part, how all returns to God through human activity. And the Third Part gives the contingent design of the return.[9] The *exitus-reditus* scheme as a basis for structuring the *Summa* was first proposed in 1939 and it soon became very popular for its elegant simplicity, and also because it matched with a dynamic and holistic salvation-history approach—which was to become dominant at Vatican II—as a substitute for the static Neo-Thomist view and its separation between philosophy and theology in Aquinas.

Chenu does not think that introducing the *exitus-reditus* scheme means imposing a pagan structure on Christian theology. He refers to Greek fathers, in particular to Pseudo-Dionysius, who adopted it. In

8. Cf. Marie-Dominique Chenu, *A School of Theology: Le Saulchoir*, trans. and ed. Joseph A. Komonchak and Mary Kate Holman (Adelaide: ATF Press, 2023), 59: "It is, then, upon history that the theologian works. His [sic] given is not the nature of things not their timeless forms; it is events, responding to an *economy* whose realization is bound to time . . . . The believer, the believing theologian, enters by faith into this plan of God, and what he seeks to understand, *quaerens intellectum*" (the emphasis is Chenu's).

9. Chenu, "Le plan de la Somme théologique de S. Thomas," *Revue thomiste* 45 (1939): 93–107. The article was translated into English as "The Plan of St. Thomas' *Summa Theologiae*," *CrossCurrents* 2, no. 2 (1952): 67–79. See also Chenu, *Toward Understanding Saint Thomas*, 306–17.

contrast to pagan neoplatonists, the Greek fathers emphasized God's freedom in creating, advocated direct participation in God (instead of emanation through intermediaries), acknowledged the temporal beginning of creation, and appreciated matter as good, created by God, and assumed by his Word.[10] Pseudo-Dionysius's *exitus-reditus* scheme provides Chenu with a particular view on participation in divine being as the basic metaphysical principle. This principle is further elaborated in the idea of the hierarchical "great chain of being."[11] Chenu characterizes Pseudo-Dionysius's worldview as follows: "The key to the understanding of the universe, and of man in the universe, was taken to be the ordered, dynamic, and progressive chain of all beings . . . in which each being is a 'theophany,' a revelation of God."[12] In this great chain of being, the top of each layer in the hierarchy of being (inanimate beings, plants, animals, human beings, angels, God) touches upon and is open toward the bottom of the layer above it. Consequently, there is a special place for the human being, the microcosmos within the hierarchy. The human being is located between the supra-rational angelic (and divine) being and infra-rational animal (and material) being. Therefore, matter and spirit, though distinct, permeate one another in this creature.[13]

The *exitus-reditus* scheme as structure of the *Summa* has been very influential. However, nowadays many Thomists no longer fully endorse it. There are textual grounds for criticizing it, for example, the fact that the end of Part One deals with God leading creatures to their goal, but also theological arguments, in particular the apparent marginalization of Christology and sacramentology, which are the subject of Part Three. I think Rudi te Velde's suggestion is very convincing that the three parts of the *Summa* are divided according to the three different agents, viz. God, human beings, and Christ. According to te Velde, the First Part is

10. Chenu, *Nature, Man, and Society in the Twelfth Century: Essays on New Theological Perspectives in the Latin West* (Chicago: University of Chicago Press, 1968), 52, 82; Chenu, "The Plan of St. Thomas' *Summa Theologiae*," 72; Chenu 1974, par. 17.

11. *The Great Chain of Being* is the title of Arthur Lovejoy's book, published in 1936, about the basic metaphysical ideas of Plato and their reception in Western thought. As far as I know, Chenu does not use the expression, but he would agree with its meaning.

12. Chenu, *Nature, Man, and Society*, 23; Chenu 1974, par. 18.

13. Chenu, *Nature, Man, and Society*, 23–25. Also Chenu 1974, par. 24.

about God and God's work of creation and world government by which everything returns to God. However, because human beings are free, they are led back to God in a special way that cannot be appropriately accounted for in terms of God's general creative agency and presence in nature. Human freedom, therefore, necessitates the Second Part on morality. Finally, the intrusion of sin into human freedom requires the Third Part on Christ's saving work and the sacraments, through which this work becomes efficacious in our lives.[14]

In general, Chenu is very sympathetic toward Aquinas and he is indebted to his way of thinking. This also goes for Chenu's views on liturgy and the sacraments.[15] However, I also think that introducing the Pseudo-Dionysian *exitus-reditus* scheme and its hierarchical chain of being obscures two main characteristics of Aquinas's sacramentology: viz. the sacrament as sign and as remedy for sin.

Symbol-Sign

Augustine's description of a sacrament as a "sacred sign" (*signum sacrum*) had become the basic category in defining sacraments for medieval scholastic theologians, including Aquinas.[16] However, Chenu is rather critical of the choice to qualify the sacrament and the sacramental as signs and he prefers the (Dionysian) category of symbol.[17]

14. See Rudi te Velde, *Aquinas on God* (Aldershot: Ashgate, 2006), 11–18. Cf. also te Velde, "Creation, Fall, and Providence," in *The Oxford Handbook of the Reception of Aquinas*, ed. Matthew Levering and Marcus Plested (Oxford: Oxford University Press, 2021), 643–57, in particular 651–54.

15. See, for example, Chenu 1967, par. 9, 22. And also his charitable reading of Aquinas's argument for limiting the number of sacraments to seven: Chenu 1952, par. 30 and Chenu 1947, par. 1.

16. D. van den Eynde, "Les définitions des sacrements pendant la première période de la théologie scolastique (1050–1235)," *Antonianum* 24, nos. 2–3 (1949): 183–228, esp. 190–99. For Augustine, see *De Civitate Dei* 10.5 (CCSL 47:277). The definition of sacrament as "sign of a sacred reality" (*signum rei sacrae*) is not found in Augustine; it appeared for the first time in the early twelfth century.

17. Chenu 1952, par. 12–14; Chenu 1967, par. 32; Chenu 1974, par. 30. Sometimes, Chenu takes "sign" in a broad sense, which includes "symbol": Chenu 1962, par. 7; Chenu 1967, par. 28. Chenu claims that Aquinas is indebted to Pseudo-Dionysius and his idea of symbol "as an 'authority' on which to base his theology of the sacraments" but he does not really justify this claim: Chenu 1967, par. 23.

It is not easy to pinpoint what Chenu's objections against "sign" as a generic category exactly are. It seems to me there are (at least) three. First, Chenu thinks that there is too much of a distinction between sign and what is signified. The sign rests upon the absence of the thing signified, while the symbol goes together with the presence of what is symbolized.[18] The second objection seems to be the main one: the sign appeals too much to human reason and its mediating role between sign (signifier) and the thing signified, while symbol is much more corporeal and emotional and immediately realizes the experience of the presence of what is symbolized.[19] The third objection is related to the previous one, and points out that the notion of "sign" suggests that what is signified can be captured in a concept and denies the supra-rational mystery.[20]

If these are indeed Chenu's main motives to prefer "symbol" over "sign," they do not apply to Aquinas's view. First, following Peter Lombard, Aquinas specifies the sacrament as a specific kind of sign, viz. a sign that causes what it signifies, an idea that had remained underdeveloped in Augustine.[21] The notion of causation secures the presence of what is signified, that is, grace and our sanctification, which is nothing but a participation by way of a kind of likeness in the divine being. In this way, Chenu's first objection is no longer valid. Of course, one can criticize the introduction of the category of cause, though we have to keep in mind that Aquinas qualifies it as a mere instrumental cause used by the risen God-human Christ, the effect of which is not

18. Chenu 1967, par. 38; Chenu 1952, par. 7, 9, 23–24. With his focus on the presence of symbolized mystery, Chenu seems to be influenced by Casel and Vonier's idea of "sacramental sacrifice" in the eucharistic celebration; the sacrifice of Christ is "re-presented," that is, becomes "sacramentally" present.

19. Chenu 1962, par. 17; Chenu 1967, par. 23, 29–30; Chenu 1974, par. 27–28. Cf. Chenu, *Toward Understanding Saint Thomas*, 310: "These Augustinian categories [scl. *res et signa, uti et frui*, HG] are centered on the psychology of man, not of the work of God as such."

20. Chenu 1952, par. 15.

21. Thomas Aquinas, *Summa Theologiae*, IIIa, q. 60, a. 3, q. 62, a. 1. Cf. Reginald Lynch, *The Cleansing of the Heart*, Thomistic Ressourcement Series, vol. 9 (Washington, DC: Catholic University of America Press, 2017), esp. 90–92. On 92 note 57, Lynch criticizes Chenu for misrepresenting the medieval reception of Augustine's *res-et-signa* distinction.

univocal.[22] Moreover, Aquinas, like most medieval theologians, thinks that the sacrament not only signifies and causes what is present, viz. habitual grace, but also signifies what is not present: it is a memorial sign of the past event of Christ's passion and death, and it points ahead to the eschatological fulfillment of our definitive sanctification. Also, Chenu mentions this threefold temporal reference, but it remains unclear how he relates it to the "presence of the mystery" in the symbol.[23]

The second objection rests on the idea that symbol belongs to the domain of reality and nature (metaphysics, ontology) rather than to the domain of knowledge and human intentionality (epistemology). In contrasting sign and symbol, Chenu writes: "The symbol, on the other hand, is a 'manifestation': it is the symbolized reality itself which, to varying degrees, asserts itself in a reality that is at the same time different and joint, and therefore at the same time exteriorizes and expresses it in it."[24]

However, for Aquinas the sacrament is first of all a sign; it is the object of our cognitive powers, both of our senses and of our rational mind. When Aquinas speaks of a *res sensibilis* (sensory reality) as part of the sacramental sign, he is not speaking metaphysically of *res materialis* as such but epistemologically of material reality insofar as it is the direct object of our sensory cognitive powers (and indirectly of our rational cognitive power). The spoken word is the other part of the sacramental sign and being a conventional, not a natural, sign, it is more immediately directed toward the rational mind. Chenu

22. Aquinas, *Summa Theologiae*, IIIa, q. 62, a. 3. In contrast, Chenu thinks that "cause" implies univocity: Chenu 1974, par. 29.

23. Chenu 1952, par. 26. In Chenu 1947, par. 14, Chenu seems to consider the threefold temporal reference as an a posteriori "conceptualization."

24. Chenu 1974, par. 27. Chenu sharply juxtaposes the Augustinian sign and the Pseudo-Dionysian symbol in *Nature, Man, and Society*, 125–26, as follows: "Augustine's 'sign' belonged on the level of his psychology of knowledge. . . . It was consequently the knower who was the principle and rule of the 'sign'; it was he who gave the 'sign' its value over and beyond any objective basis in the nature of things . . . For pseudo-Dionysius, it was not the believer who gave signs their meaning; it was objective elements themselves which . . . were so many representations. . . . The symbol was the true and proper expression of reality; nay more, it was through such symbolization that reality fulfilled itself."

acknowledges that human beings are rational: "The human, certainly, is reason; to deviate from reason, or even to mistrust it, is to run the risk of becoming dehumanized."[25] However, he immediately seems to split reason into the (infra-rational) sensible and the (supra-rational) intelligence: "But reason is precisely defined as an intelligence immersed in the sensible."[26] While for Aquinas dynamic discursive reason (*ratio*) is the specifically human way of being that bridges the gap between the sensory perception of the material world and intuitive intelligence (*intellectus*) of the intelligible world,[27] Chenu gives the impression of blowing up this bridge and of denying the intermediary role of reason: the symbol is the immediate leap (*saut*) from the sensory, the material world, to the transcendent mystery, the spiritual world of intuitive, nonconceptual intelligence.[28] Occasionally, Chenu mentions the spoken words as the other part of the sacrament besides the sensory element. In Aquinas's sacramentology, spoken words are essential for semiotic reasons: they determine the polysemy of the sensory element.[29] However, Chenu minimalizes their cognitive role. He emphasizes that they are words of *faith* but ignores the importance of the rational meaning or conceptual content of these spoken words.[30] Rational conceptualizations, whether by the theologian or the ordinary believer, are only secondary, a posteriori, critical activities.

When expressing the third objection, Chenu acknowledges the role of analogy, that is the logical doctrine that the meaning of a word can be expanded beyond its primary significate. But in Chenu's eyes, analogy does not do enough justice to God's transcendence.[31] Maybe

25. Chenu 1967, par. 31. See also Chenu 1947, par. 5. In Chenu 1974, par. 24, Chenu mentions Aquinas's anthropology in which the human being appears as a "microcosmos" but Chenu seems to consider the "junction of matter and spirit" as rather extrinsic.

26. Chenu 1967, par. 31.

27. Cf. J. Peghaire, *Intellectus et ratio selon s. Thomas d'Aquin* (Paris: Vrin, 1936).

28. Chenu 1967, par. 36. See also Chenu 1947, par. 4, 14; and Chenu 1962, par. 16.

29. Aquinas, *Summa Theologiae*, III, q. 60, a. 6. Aquinas also mentions the parallels with the incarnation of the Word and with the hylomorphic composition of the human being.

30. Chenu 1962, par. 6–7.

31. Chenu 1952, par. 15.

Chenu was still too much influenced by Cajetan's interpretation of analogy in Aquinas and by the dominant role of the so-called *analogia proportionalitatis,* which tends to neglect the incommensurability between God and creatures. However this may be, for Aquinas himself analogy serves to safeguard God's otherness. When a noun (e.g., "just" or "being") is predicated of God, Aquinas writes, "[T]he thing signified is left as something that is uncomprehended and that exceeds the signification of the noun."[32]

Sacrament and Original Sin

The predominance of the *exitus-reditus* scheme also distorts the role of (original) sin in Aquinas's sacramentology. Again, it is a certain anti-Augustinian sentiment that is in the background. Chenu contrasts Augustine's and Pseudo-Dionysius's views on the role and necessity of the sacraments as follows: "[T]he Augustinian bias that led to considering the sacraments as so many remedies for a fallen world, remedies that would not have existed in a world without the fall, where with matter properly subjected to spirit, man's understanding would not have had to make use of matter in the worship of God. In realist symbolism, on the contrary, including that of Pseudo-Dionysius, symbolic action is a normal part of a dynamism of a cosmos reaching upward toward God in hierarchical stages."[33]

Aquinas gives three reasons why sacraments are necessary.[34] The first one lies in the natural constitution of the human being as a unity of body and spirit, that is, as an embodied soul or an ensouled body. The second reason is (original) sin, and the third our proclivity toward corporeal actions, which runs the risk of leading to magical and superstitious practices. It is remarkable that Chenu reverses the order and says that Aquinas mentions the sacraments as remedies against (original) sin as third and that he was the only theologian of his time

32. Aquinas, *Summa Theologiae,* I, q. 13, a. 5.

33. Chenu, *Nature, Man, and Society,* 135. However, in Chenu 1974, par. 26, Chenu seems to endorse the idea that there were no sacraments in the prelapsarian state of humanity.

34. Aquinas, *Summa Theologiae,* III, q. 61, a. 1.

not to put "remedy against sin" in the first place. "Here," Chenu writes, referring to sacraments as remedy against (original) sin, "we leave the order of natures and the emanation of being to move on to a reflection from Augustinianism."[35] Chenu downplays the importance of (original) sin both in Aquinas's and in his own view on the sacraments. However, it is evident that for Aquinas (original) sin plays a crucial role in the sacraments. Aquinas states that before the fall there was no need for sacraments, not for healing the wounds of sin (which is obvious), but also not for elevating our natural being to the supernatural level.[36] In other words, Aquinas thinks our natural constitution as a material-spiritual composite is only a necessary and not a sufficient condition for the existence of sacraments; the reality of original sin is also required. Chenu, on the other hand, thinks that Aquinas bases the existence of the sacraments on "a naturalistic principle" with (supernatural) deification as their raison d'être. Human nature as created, not as fallen, already asks for sacraments in order to reach union with God.[37]

The Pseudo-Dionysian symbol and its background in the *exitus-reditus* scheme leaves very little room for (original) sin as an obstacle in the movement of creation to God. As mentioned above, one of the theological objections against imposing this scheme on the *Summa Theologiae* is that it leads to a marginalization of the Third Part, which deals with Christ and the sacraments. The fact that Chenu depreciates the forgiveness for (original) sin in his sacramentology strengthens this objection.

There are at least three possible reasons why Chenu ignores the role of (original) sin in the sacraments. One is the general tendency in Catholic theology after Trent to regard the fall as the mere loss of the supernatural (and preternatural) gift of original righteousness and to

35. Chenu 1974, par. 4. Cf. Chenu 1974, par. 31: "[T]he sin of sacramental Augustinianism in scholasticism is to leave aside creation, when instead the incarnation must find its full value in it." This statement suggests a Scotist instead of a Thomist "motive" for the incarnation. Aquinas thinks that if there were no sin, the incarnation would not have happened: *Summa Theologiae*, III, q. 1, a. 3.

36. *Summa Theologiae*, III, q. 61, a. 2.

37. Chenu 1974, par. 9 (cf. also par. 14). See also Chenu 1967, par. 22; and Chenu 1962, par. 15.; cf. *Summa Theologiae*, III, q. 61, a. 2.

deny that original sin has any effects on human nature itself. A second one is the optimism with regard to human capacities that prevailed in the period around Vatican II. Third, the doctrine of original sin is a hallmark of Western, Augustinian theology and does not play an important role in Greek theology, which influenced Chenu so much.

Conclusion

Chenu's texts on liturgy and sacraments are not always very clear and they are more nuanced and less systematic than I suggested in my analysis. And Chenu and Aquinas also have much in common. Nevertheless, we can conclude that Aquinas is much more indebted to Augustine in his sacramentology than Chenu thinks. The predominance Chenu gives to Pseudo-Dionysius's *exitus-reditus* scheme and his notion of symbol obscures (1) how Aquinas takes sacraments primarily as signs and (2) the role he attributes to sacraments as remedies for (original) sin.

From a historical point of view, Chenu has not been loyal to Aquinas's thought about the sacraments. As he had already mentioned in his doctoral thesis, Chenu wanted to "understand the thought of St. Thomas in the milieu in which it was born."[38] However, he situated Aquinas more in a neoplatonic world of late antiquity and the early Middle Ages than in the Augustinian-Aristotelian world of the thirteenth century. But how bad is this for systematic theology? We should definitely appreciate Chenu's efforts to rectify an unembodied, spiritualized, and formalized performance and experience of liturgy and sacraments, but I think that the two issues I discussed also show that Chenu sacrifices important theological insights.

With regard to the first point, symbol versus sign, the main issue is whether we should consider sacraments primarily within a metaphysical or within an epistemological framework. Keeping in mind that the sign includes both sensory elements and words, an advantage of the latter option is that sacraments are treated as human activity, filled with intentionality, consciousness, and rationality.

38. See the quotation on p. 149 above.

With regard to the second point, Chenu emphasizes that he wants a dialogue between theology of the sacraments and the social sciences (*sciences humaines*).[39] Theology, he thinks, should respect the full autonomy of the social sciences for theological reasons. However, one could question the conditions for such a dialogue and the validity of the autonomy of the social sciences within the domain of theology. The very idea of human nature being intrinsically wounded by original sin and in need of healing grace falls beyond the scope of the social sciences but is crucial, in my view (and Aquinas's), for any theological anthropology.

39. Chenu 1947, par. 2; Chenu 1967, par. 2; Chenu 1974, par. 5–6.

The Symbolic Gesture, Moved by Mystery

Willem Marie Speelman

In "Anthropology and Liturgy" (1947) Marie-Dominique Chenu describes the liturgy as an encounter between the "supra-rational" mystery and the "infra-rational" symbol, in which the symbol is said to represent the mystery.[1] The words "supra-rational" and "infra-rational" place the mystery and the symbol at the borders of the human reality. There is something "up" there and there is something "down" here, both of which we cannot grasp, and which are brought into a mutual relationship in the liturgy through the mediation of the mystery and the symbol. The unknown "up" there I will call God, who revealed Godself to Moses as Presence (Exod 3:14), and the unknown "down" here will be the living flesh, which is our own invisible (sic!) presence.[2] Chenu stresses the fact that the liturgical *mise-en-relation* of the mystery and the symbol is done by the human being, in the human history and the human language. The believed effect of their encounter is the communication ("expression and transmission") of grace in the human reality.

1. Chenu 1947, par. 4.

2. Note that life itself is invisible, that you cannot see your seeing. Life is the breath with which God made the human live: the Word made flesh. Cf. Michel Henry, *Incarnation: A Philosophy of Flesh*, trans. Karl Hefty (Evanston, IL: Northwestern University Press, 2015), 14: "Thus it is by identifying himself with the Word's flesh . . . that the man . . . may identify himself with God"; and on page 19: "The definition of an invisible, and at the same time carnal, human being—and invisible in so far as carnal."

I will try to follow the path of Chenu in the articulation of this relationship between the mystery and the symbol, how humans perform their liturgical *mise-en-relation* and what it does to the human reality. Along the way I will quote other authors, who shed light on particular questions in this process.

- I will argue that the relationship of mystery and symbol brings about a mutual transformation of the participants in this relationship (Chenu calls this "a reciprocal request and a mutual safeguard"),[3] and I will identify this mutual transformation as the spiritual process.
- The human action of the *mise-en-relation,* a celebration, will be described as a gesture. A gesture is a distinct type of action, next to doing and making, an action of which the effect is not in our hands. As its effect is not in the hands of the actor, faith functions in the gesture: that it will work in itself as it is performed by the human.
- In the mutual transformation—which is believed to be happening, not done—the symbol expresses and represents the mystery, which thus becomes the content of the symbol. But following the critique of Chenu on the sign relationship of signifier and signified, I will propose a musical semiotic approach of this representation. The mutual transformation can be described in the musical term of "resonance" (although Chenu uses the word "analogy"). In music, it is the material that communicates, not matter as such, but as it is sensed by the human flesh (*res sensibilis*).
- I will close my argument with the proposition that the symbol can be recognized as bearing the signatures of the participants of the encounter.

Sacer, Sanctus, and the Profane

We need to make clear what the "sacred domain" is, in which the mystery and the symbol hold their ultimate and in a sense "defining"

3. Chenu 1947, par. 14.

positions *supra* and *infra* the human reality. The question of the sacred has been discussed by Émile Benveniste, who distinguishes between the Latin words *sacer* and *sanctus*. *Sanctus* is the sanctified, a holiness made explicit by the impending sanction of its desecration. The implied holiness, that is sanctified by *sanctus*, is expressed in the word *sacer*.[4] Human action, for example, in the liturgy, sanctifies to define that which cannot be grasped, as it is *sacer*. In the words of Giorgio Agamben, *sacer* is the exclusive, which by human action is "included" in the human reality "through an exclusion."[5] It is something or someone set apart. Chenu's words *supra* and *infra* can therefore be interpreted as the mystery and the symbol representing the sacred set apart in the human reality as the divine sovereign—God's presence—and bare life—the invisible presence of our living flesh.

If grace is communicated in the liturgy, it will be communicated between both ends of the sacred, God's Presence and our own presence in the flesh, in their mutual interaction. Both presences are only expressible insofar as they are implied by the words and actions. The words and actions will be described here as the approach of reality as a mystery and the approach of realities as symbols.

The relationship with *sacer* through the mediation of the holy mystery and the holy symbols involves human activity. But the activity of presence itself, God's presence and the presence of our living flesh, is not an activity that human beings can own and control. I have no control over my body healing a wound, growing hair, and digesting

4. Émile Benveniste, *Dictionary of Indo-European Concepts and Society* (Chicago: Hau Books, 2016), 463–65: "There is not only the difference between *sacer* as a natural state and *sanctus* as the result of some operation. One said: *via sacra, mons sacer, dies sacra*, but always *murus sanctus, lex sancta*. What is *sanctus* is the wall and not the domain enclosed by it, which is said to be *sacer*. What is *sanctus* is what is defended by certain sanctions. But the fact of making contact with the 'sacred' does not bring about the state of being *sanctus*. There is no sanction for the man who by touching the *sacer* himself becomes *sacer*. He is banished from the community, but he is not punished any more than the man who kills him is. One might say of the *sanctum* that it is what is found on the periphery of the *sacrum*, what serves to isolate it from all contact."

5. Giorgio Agamben, *Homo Sacer: Sovereign Power and Bare Life*, in Agamben, *The Omnibus Homo Sacer: Homo Sacer I*, 1–159 (Stanford, CA: Stanford University Press, 2017), 12.

food, nor can I make God answer my prayer. The important activity happens in the relationship itself and transforms all participants of this relationship. Kees Waaijman has identified this transformational process in the mutual involvement of the divine and the human as the spiritual process.[6] In a way, the mystery and the symbol work in itself, as they are performed in the liturgical actions: they change everything.

The Mystery as a Distinct Reality, Forming the *Sacer*

Although Chenu is not clear in his understanding of the word "mystery"—in a footnote he calls it a "sacred action, containing, in some way, grace"[7]—his approach is in line with the way Gabriel Marcel and Karl Rahner write about it. Mystery is a positive reality[8]—opposed to the negative "what we do not yet know"—which is to be approached in the way in which this reality presents itself to the human: by responding to its presence with our own presence.[9] If a faithful person bows before the altar, his or her gesture is the responding faith of Christ's presence in that thing. Marcel distinguishes the mystery as alternative to the worldly problem-solution approach of reality. A problem wants to be solved—for example, the poor man who is standing in our way—whereas the mystery calls into presence—for example, by engaging in an encounter with this man as if he were Christ. Chenu touches this distinction in several places, for example, when he criticizes the question of causality and the tendency to explain the mystery, which are both examples of a problem-solving strategy: "What caused this?" and "What does it mean?" Mystery—nor symbol, for that matter—does

6. Kees Waaijman, *Spiritualiteit. Vormen, Grondslagen, Methoden* (Kampen: Kok / Gent: Carmelitana, 2000), 424.

7. Chenu 1947, footnote 1.

8. Karl Rahner, "The Concept of Mystery in Catholic Theology," in *Theological Investigations*, vol. 4, trans. Kevin Smyth (London: Darton, Longman and Todd, 1966), 36–73, here 41: "an 'unknowing' . . . a positive characteristic of a relationship between one subject and another."

9. Gabriel Marcel, *The Mystery of Being: I. Reflection & Mystery* (Chicago: Henry Regnery, 1950), 204: "Perhaps the shortest way towards our needed definition of the notion of mystery would be to begin by working out the distinction, at the spiritual level, between what we call an *object* and what we call a *presence*."

not call for a rational explanation, but wants to be approached in faithfulness and truthfulness: "Who are you?" If one would ask what a mystery means, one would have to take a distance and describe it as an object; but mystery generates meaning in the encounter only.

Marcel distinguishes the mystery in any reality, and believes that every problem conceals a mystery.[10] According to Rahner mystery ultimately refers to God,[11] so that every mystery we meet, for example in any creature, is also an invitation to an encounter with its Creator. Chenu includes every human action, when he writes: "As St. Thomas observes, all human behavior will be made sacred at the very moment when the unique and irreducible originality of the mystery captures the slightest action for its own benefit."[12] The point here is that mystery can only be met by a different approach, by responding to its presence with your own presence, and that the initiative of this encounter lies with the mystery, which presents itself to you. We will recognize this mystery approach in the symbol later, but my next step is to interpret the approach itself as a distinct type of human action: a gesture.

The Gesture as a Distinct Action

Terrentius Varro distinguishes the verb *gerere* as a third type of action, next to *facere* (making) and *agere* (doing).[13] *Gerere*—from which gesture and gestation are derived—means to bear, to carry out, and to demonstrate. What does a woman do when she is carrying a child? She is not making the child or performing its growth, but she is bodily following the movement of her child's growing and eventually being born. Likewise, the gesture is a type of action in which the performer does not own the act or its effect by doing or making it. They serve someone else's action, for example by doing it in his or her name. I

10. Gabriel Marcel, *Being and Having*, trans. Katharine Farrer (Westminster: Dacre Press, 1949), 111.

11. Rahner, "Concept of Mystery in Catholic Theology," 54.

12. Chenu 1952, par. 31. When an interviewer asked the American composer John Cage: "If I open this door, is it art?" the composer answered: "If you celebrate it."

13. Terenzio Varrone, *De lingua latina*, A cure di Emilio Piccolo (Napoli: Classici Latini Loffredo, 2009), 49. See https://www.academia.edu/33321912/Marco_Terenzio_Varrone_De_lingua_latina_pdf (accessed April 25, 2024).

will tentatively describe the gesture as the performance of an act, to be recognized as belonging to another actor, with the intention of evoking a different reality before the eyes of witnesses.[14] The works of mercy are symbolic actions which represent the mystery of God's mercy, but they do not rid the world of its problems.

The approach of mystery and symbol as gestures shows that they are actions rather than things. Let us concentrate on the act of symbolizing for the moment. If we approach symbol as an act, the act turns a reality—any reality—into a symbol. In the article "For a Sacramental Anthropology" (1974) Chenu writes that it is not matter in itself, abstracted from any relation, nor matter as an element in the cosmos, abstracted from any intelligibility, but that the symbol—or in this case, the sacrament—has as its essential component matter as *res sensibilis,* that is, matter as it is sensed by the human body.[15] The material of a symbol is matter insofar as I sense its effect, its imprint in my living flesh. To sense is, however passive it may seem, a human activity. Truly seeing someone is not the same thing as staring in his or her direction, and the same is true for tasting water. Sensing is a gesture in which the human subject bears the presence of the sensed person or matter.

But the symbolic gesture also transforms the human subject, for his and her living flesh bears the presence of another person or thing. The Constitution on the Sacred Liturgy writes that "when a man baptizes it is really Christ Himself who baptizes."[16] This is the meaning of the symbol as a re-presentation, a bearing of the presence, of the mystery of our own flesh as well as the mystery of Christ.

The transformation of the human subject is an initiation. Discussing the importance of initiation in "Faith and Sacrament," Chenu writes that "initiation is the operation by which faith realizes, through symbolic action, communion with the mystery."[17] Whose faith? To a large extent faith is given in the gesture of performing the divine Word, just as, for example, people believe in a story when it is told in a trustworthy

14. See, for a discussion, Giorgio Agamben, *Karman: A Brief Treatise on Action, Guilt, and Gesture* (Stanford, CA: Stanford University Press, 2018); see also my "Pope Francis and Francis of Assisi: Men of Gesture," *Franciscan Studies* 78 (2020): 275–88.

15. Chenu 1974, par. 16.

16. *Sacrosanctum Concilium* 7. See https://www.vatican.va/archive/hist_councils/ii_vatican_council/documents/vat-ii_const_19631204_sacrosanctum-concilium_en.html.

17. Chenu 1962, par. 12.

way. We have seen that the spiritual process of mutual transformation happens in a gesture and is not done or made: my faith alone does not make my prayer effective. Initiation (from *in-ire*, entering into) happens when someone truly enters into the liturgy, and responds with faith to the faith given. The transformation happens in a relationship, and therefore the communion is realized by a shared faith.

Quoting Augustine, Chenu writes that the word approaching (or being added to) the matter makes the sacrament as a visible word (*"accedit verbum ad elementum, et fit sacramentum, etiam ipsum tanquam visibile verbum"*), whereby he identifies the word (*verbum*) as the profession of faith.[18] But the profession of faith, *symbolon*, is a response to the Word of God, a moving along with the act of Christ. In the symbolic act of the blessing of the water, for example, it is not our faith—which may be imperfect or even false—but the Word of God proclaimed over the water, which transforms the water into a visible word.[19] In the gesture both participants are needed, the Word of the present One and the responding faith of our own presence. In "Faith and Sacrament" (1962) Chenu stresses that "they must in no way seem to be dissociated."[20]

The gesture of symbolization evokes a different reality before the eyes of witnesses, which is more than a sign can do. Where a sign indicates a different reality, the symbol reveals its activity. In Chenu's example of the Word of God as a seed—and not: "like" a seed—the symbol tells us something about the act of the word, not about its being.[21]

The Symbol as a Distinct Sign

We have referred to Marcel's distinction of a mystery approach to the reality on the one hand, and the modern problem-solving approach on the other. In a comparable way, the symbol is distinct from (the modern understanding of) the sign. Chenu criticizes the approach of the symbol as a sign. To clarify his position, I want to mention the

18. Chenu 1962, par. 7.

19. Jan Lemmens, "De Sacramenten en het Vleesgeworden Woord volgens Augustinus," *Augustiniana* 14 (1964): 5–71, here 30.

20. Chenu 1962, par. 9.

21. Chenu 1962, par. 32.

sign theory of Ferdinand de Saussure, which he seems to oppose.[22] According to Saussure a sign is a form, exclusively defined by negative relations between opposites: A is not-B and B is not-A. And indeed, the term "symbol" has also been used in this abstract way, as for example in mathematics. The question of defining the symbol was never solved,[23] but the point is that the sign theory approaches the symbol as a problem. As a sign, the symbol could be analyzed in detail, and this analysis would lead to the solution of the problem of its signification. Any solution based on oppositions would lead to a discussion, an explanation, and an understanding. But these are all terms that Chenu rejects as fitting the symbol.

One of the difficulties met with the sign theory is that the form, abstracted from any substance (matter), disengages the sign from the human being or any other reality. In linguistics, the user of the sign is defined exclusively by its formal categories, *énonciateur* vs. *énonciataire,* in such a way that *énonciateur* is not *énonciataire, énonciataire* is not author, *énonciataire* is not listener or reader. In fact, every aspect of the reality in which the sign functions is appropriated by the sign system and redefined in pure oppositions (leaving the reality outside its scope). Thus, language creates its own closed and abstract reality, an object of research and a problem to be solved. As a result, the reality of mystery, or any reality that refuses to be appropriated by the system, cannot be described as a sign in the strict semiotic sense.

However, language is not the only medium of communication. A semiotics of music may shed light on the symbol as a distinct sign. Unlike language, music is not built on oppositions but on proportions.[24] We find proportions in the names for the material of music:

22. Ferdinand de Saussure, *Cours de linguistique Générale* (Paris: Payot, 1972). I am describing his sign theory, which has been very influential in the twentieth century. Saussure differentiates the symbol from the sign as a relationship that is not arbitrary: "il n'est pas vide, il y a un rudiment de lien naturel entre le significant et le signifié" (101).

23. "Symbol," in *Historische Wörterbuch der Philosophie* (Darmstadt: Wissenschaftliche Buchgesellschaft, 1989), k. 735.

24. Willem Marie Speelman, "Woorden kunnen worden verstaan, muziek moet worden gevolgd. Taal en muziek als fundamentele categorieën van de liturgie," in Martin Hoondert et al. (red.), *Elke muziek heeft haar hemel. De religieuze betekenis van muziek* (Budel: Damon, 2009), 161–83. Or Speelman, "The Meaning of Music in

an interval is a proportion (e.g., the fifth is the proportion 3:2), a duration is expressed by a proportion (e.g., a quarter note is the proportion 1:4), and the dynamics are a proportionate loudness expressed in a scale from *pianissimo* to *fortissimo* (not the opposition soft vs. loud). From this proportionality of the musical material all other characteristics of the musical semiotics derive. Let me gather some important characteristics:

- Perceiving musical proportions—intervals, rhythms, dynamics—consists in tuning in to them and letting them move your body, starting with your ears. Therefore, music generates meaning not by referring to something else, but by resonating with the music itself. When the *dies irae* motif is heard in a symphony, the motif is not referring to the *dies irae* but resounding it. Is this not the way a symbol leaves an imprint in the living flesh, "I sense water, God's water" that is expressed in *res sensibilis*?
- As music is perceived by resonating with its proportions, musical "understanding" is not an explanation but a following, as in "I am following this melodic line." Is this not the way in which liturgy is celebrated, by following the ritual program?
- As music is followed by the body, music does not disengage from the body or the environment, but instead the body and the environment resound the music. Is this not the "symbol [as] the expression immediately homogeneous to the mystery" in which we are initiated according to Chenu?[25]
- As musical communication consists in resounding the movement into which the listener enters, the reception of its "message" is a growing participation with the movement in the place where the music is sounding. Is this not a proper description of a liturgical celebration as an active participation?

Christian Faith," in Maeve Heaney and Bennett Zon, eds., *Oxford Handbook of Music and Christian Theology*, vol. 1 (forthcoming).

25. Chenu 1962, par. 13.

All these musical relations can be recognized in the description of the symbol as a distinct sign. The sign divides content from expression; the symbol is undivided ("bears its reference"). The sign indicates; the symbol re-presents. The sign is produced by the brain; the symbol, sensed by the flesh. The sign disengages the user from the world; the symbol calls for his or her presence and transforms him or her into a symbol. When 800 years ago Francis of Assisi wondered what the meaning of his vision of the Seraph might be, he received—as a response—the wounds of Christ in his body, and became a symbol of Christ.[26] There is an example of symbolic communication!

Chenu understands the symbolic signification, which I described as resonance, in terms of analogy as a distinct form of reference. The symbol bears its reference which impresses the living flesh. One can compare it with a string of the violin bearing the movement of the other string and representing this same movement with its own colors. In the same way as the mystery is not a negative (*not* yet revealed) but a positive truth of the Unknown (Karl Rahner), a symbol is a positive means conveying its message by analogy: a mutual relationship in which the one and the other realities both resound. Or in the words of Paul Ricœur on the functioning of symbols: "Cosmos and Psyche are the two poles of the same 'expressivity'; I express myself in expressing the world; I explore my own sacrality in deciphering that of the world."[27]

In the examples given above, we may recognize the original meaning of the symbol as identifier, by the fitting together of two parts forming a whole (like a broken ring put together). Only in this case, the whole was not split in the past, but the two (or more) parts are transformed toward each another. In the gesture of symbolization, all the participants enter into a mutual transformation, in which the one becomes symbol of the other, the one a mystery for the other. Thus, the symbol is one part signifying another, without any of them being a sign in the strict linguistic sense of the word. The symbol can be better described as a signature.

26. *The Life of Saint Francis by Thomas of Celano,* 94, in *Francis of Assisi: Early Documents, vol. 1, The Saint,* ed. Regis J. Armstrong, J. A. Wayne Hellmann, and William J. Short (New York: New City Press, 1999), 264. See https://franciscantradition.org/earlysources (accessed April 25, 2024).

27. Paul Ricœur, *The Symbolism of Evil* (Boston: Beacon Press, 1969), 13.

The Signature

What Chenu has not mentioned but can be recognized in his discussions is the domain of signature. To begin with, there is hesitation in Chenu's words when he writes: "the symbol is for the initiated more than a simple sign, for . . . here the reference is carried by the very material of the symbol, in its gravity, I would even say, in its flesh."[28] The "flesh" of the symbol elicits the Word becoming flesh in John 1:14. The matter from which the symbol, for example, the crucifix, is made, seems wood or stone or metal. But when it, through the gesture of symbolization, becomes a symbol, its matter is that which is sensed by the living flesh, and thus transformed. The sensible thing—for example, the trembling string—meets the sensing flesh—for example, the listening ear—and their relationship realizes the material of the symbol. The ear values the trembling string by receiving it as a tone. The human flesh gives the trembling string its meaning.

If we continue this metaphor, the value of tone is given by the music, for example, of Johann Sebastian Bach. This means that there is another pole in the relationship, which values the material of the symbol. When Chenu writes in 1967: "More than 'form,' 'matter' is, so to speak, the living flesh of the sacraments," he refers in a footnote to the *Summa Theologiae* IIIa, q. 60, a. 4.[29] In the referred question, Thomas argues that things can be known on the basis of their sensible effects, and further, that the sensible things in the sacraments receive their intelligibility as spiritual things from other signs. In 1974 Chenu calls this "an intelligibility different from matter," which "influence[s] the intelligibility of the sacrament."[30] Chenu continues his discussion by describing a neoplatonic understanding of participation. I would rather meditate a little longer on his approach of the matter as "the living flesh of the sacrament," for the sensing of the flesh may be a human signature for the value and meaning of the symbol.

One of the meanings of the Greek *symbolon* is a contract, and a contract bears two signatures. According to Giorgio Agamben, the signature does not coincide with the sign, but is "what makes the sign

28. Chenu 1962, par. 17.
29. Chenu 1967, par. 18.
30. Chenu 1974, par. 16.

intelligible."[31] The signature gives things their value, so that you listen to the music differently when you recognize Bach and you value the liturgy differently when you recognize the signature of Christ. But also, and Chenu does not stop stressing this, you can only value the music and the liturgy when you are touched by it in your whole bodily being. This means that your own signature is needed.

The intelligibility of things and persons is guaranteed by signatures. The sensing flesh puts the signature of the human being on the symbol, whereas the Word made flesh can be considered as the signature of the divine. *Signare* is the root of the word "blessing" in German (*segnen*) and Dutch (*zegenen*), and together with the sign of the cross, the Word of God is the signature that is given in the ritual of the blessing. And when a faithful participant receives the material of the symbol in his or her flesh, by truly sensing it and thus valuing it, this is his or her signature. The symbol bears the signatures of both presences in the spiritual relationship, which transforms all participants. And as music moves the entire reality in which it is played, does this not also apply to the liturgy? If anything can become a symbol and any creature can be approached as a mystery, would the celebration of the liturgy be reserved for the closed space of a church, or is there liturgy around us?

A Cosmic Liturgy

Chenu closes his discussion with a perspective on a cosmic liturgy. When human beings celebrate their liturgy, they participate in a liturgy which is already being celebrated, not only in other churches and other countries, but first of all in heaven.[32] Chenu warns against an "angelic" hieraticism, which would indeed disengage us from our human flesh.[33] But what if the "heavenly" movements resound in our flesh, and move us?

In 2025, it was 800 years ago that Francis of Assisi taught his brothers to sing the *Canticle of the Creatures*. This song is an excellent

31. Giorgio Agamben, *The Signature of All Things: On Method* (New York: Zone Books, 2009), 42.

32. *Sacrosanctum Concilium* 8.

33. Chenu 1974, par. 33.

example of a cosmic liturgy, for it is an earthly response to, or better, a resounding of the heavenly choirs. Francis does not mention the angels, or even Christ, but resounds the good qualities of the bodies of heaven (sun, moon, stars), the bodies of the earth (air, water, fire, earth) and the bodies of people ("those who . . . " and our bodily death). The cosmos is not in me, but—just like the mystery in the view of Marcel—in and around me: as a multitude of brothers and sisters, who bear their origin and goal in the Creator, and who allow the human being to participate in this one movement of praise.

Perspectives from Feminist Theology

Susan K. Roll

When I began this study of Chenu's thought on sacraments and liturgy as expressed in these articles, I was delighted to see traces of the work of one of my Leuven instructors, a mentor and an old friend: Christiane Brusselmans. Dr. Brusselmans (1930–1991) was a leading figure worldwide in the development and implementation of the Rite of Christian Initiation of Adults. Chenu does not cite her name, and they may have been doing research on parallel, not interlinked, tracks, on the Rite of Christian Initiation of Adults.[1] Nonetheless, I recognized the roots of the historical research that was done in the 1950s and 60s around the ancient shape of the rite. More importantly, those researchers were thinking pastorally and proactively about what such a rite to prepare candidates for baptism could look like today. Briefly, it would provide a stronger, more authentic, and deeply-rooted experiential journey toward Christian initiation, quite different from a purely catechetical approach, yet leading to the same sacraments. Even more, such a way of escorting adult candidates for baptism into the church could not only build a solid foundation for a lifelong personal faith, but would be part of a wide-scale renewal of parishes and the

1. Dr. Brusselmans published primarily catechetical material and explanatory descriptions of the catechumenal process, although her doctoral dissertation from 1965 dealt with the role of sponsors in the ancient rite. See Catherine Dooley and Lisa Gulino, "Christiane Brusselmans," https://www.biola.edu/talbot/ce20/database/christiane-brusselmans (accessed January 29, 2024). Chenu treats the catechumenal process in 1964, esp. par. 3, 4, 12, 13.

church as a whole, as parishioners accompanied the catechumens on their journey to explore the faith and their parish community, and to find themselves in it.

My topic, however, is a feminist approach to Chenu's vision and theology. While Dr. Brusselmans was a pioneer who had to contend with a variety of forms of discrimination against women in Roman Catholic academic theology, including in Leuven, she would not have thought to self-identify as a feminist. Moreover, I would say, the church as she knew it, the church into which the RCIA would initiate those who were attracted to its rich traditions and warm companionship, has been sharply diminished today. The pressure of continual revelations of clergy abuse of vulnerable persons, frustration with the slow pace of reform to welcome persons of any gender, and a perception of irrelevance leading to simple indifference have contributed to a wave of church-leaving in many countries, not limited to the Catholic Church, coupled with an increase in the visibility of church reform groups and a marked movement to the margins of parish liturgical and sacramental practice.

Introductory Notes on Feminist Thinking around Liturgy and Sacraments

Feminist theology, as we know, is a method of analysis that raises very new questions and takes often startling approaches based on lived experience, the sharing of that experience, critical research, and creative new thinking. At the same time, the Women's Liturgical Movement, or Feminist Liturgical Movement, began already in the 1970s with a proliferation of ritual experimentation among groups of women. Some of the issues that marked the shape of feminist liturgy, such as inclusive language,[2] a creation-centered approach, and a wider range of metaphors for God, have gradually been taken up into official liturgies in various denominations.

2. Marjorie Procter-Smith distinguishes sexist, inclusive, and emancipatory language in *In Her Own Rite: Constructing Feminist Liturgical Tradition* (Nashville: Abingdon, 1990), 52–71.

More significantly, however, the guiding principles of feminist liturgical practice of the first thirty years have been increasingly employed in the liturgical celebrations of base communities and church reform organizations, large and small, in which all participants are welcome regardless of gender. The earlier focus on expansion of symbols and metaphors has broadened to a cosmic spirituality embedded in ritual; textual resources include poetry as well as the indigenous New Testament and a variety of inclusive lectionaries and Scripture resources; the social justice dimension has expanded as well to participate in networks of activists confronting larger global issues of justice. Leadership in liturgy has always expanded the number of speakers and preachers beyond a single presider, and now the expansion is fully incorporated into such liturgies, including women presiders and preachers who would not be permitted in the official liturgies of the Roman Catholic Church. Music, art, and bodily movement continue to encompass a wider, more inclusive approach. The proliferation of live-stream liturgies that began with the pandemic shutdown has been embraced by a number of Catholic reform groups because of the possibility to expand the range of participants beyond those physically present in a room, literally to a worldwide reach. Shared homily discussions in breakout rooms promote enriching international and intercultural dialogue within a shared context of prayer and rite.

The distinction between liturgies and paraliturgies used by Chenu in the 1947 article has long since disappeared. Yet the rest of Chenu's sentence describing a 1946 celebration at Colombes stadium, "a kind of creative imagination charged with expressing the collective emotion of the moment on a traditional basis."[3] nicely characterizes the new forms of ritual prayer and devotion developing at the margins of the church—the growing edge, if you will—and moving bit by bit toward the center. This makes perfect sense when one considers to what degree adaptation and reform of the liturgy historically begins at the grassroots level—study of the sources, attention to pastoral needs, awareness of the spiritual needs of the cultural context of the time, and the passion to bring about social justice for the poor and disadvantaged. Eventually authentic reform initiatives seep into policy.

3. Chenu 1947, par. 26.

For our purposes here, I have selected four aspects of Chenu's thought in these articles: symbolism, the nature of tradition (or Tradition), the inculturation of the liturgy, and the nature of history and the contemporary interpretation of ancient sources.

Symbolism

Chenu's validation of symbol and the access it grants to mystery stands out particularly in his 1952 and 1962 articles. In 1952 he wrote, "The symbol is not an ornamental accessory of the mystery, nor a provisional pedagogy, it is the co-essential resource of its communication. . . . Such is the bond of mystery and symbol."[4] His understanding and articulation of the profundity of the spiritual depth to which the symbol gives access is breathtaking. A faith that focuses only on verbal expression and cognitive understanding misses so much.

The centrality of symbol, whether a physical object, the symbolic arrangement of ritual space, symbolism in music or dance, or the symbolism of poetic words whose meaning resonates beyond the merely indicative data-driven content: all of this was a principle in early feminist liturgical experimentation. The women who had grown restless with exclusion, belittling stereotypes, and only cramped roles permitted to them, found the richness they knew lay under the surface of their faith in creative uncovering of new symbols and unfolding their potential layers of significance.

What this means, however, is that this spiritual need and drive necessarily moves beyond the concept that all symbols employed in Christian liturgy or sacraments are pre-assigned with a defined range of meaning content. Reading past the rewarding richness of Chenu's restoration of the centrality of symbol is a presumption of the givenness of symbol: "it is based on a revealed given."[5] Chenu eloquently affirms the natural character of the symbols used in liturgical celebration, yet if symbols depend ultimately upon divine revelation, what does this mean in practice? Is there a danger that forms of human domination and control could be read into, and be justified, as dependence

4. Chenu 1952, par. 13.
5. Chenu 1952, par. 32.

on revelation? This may be partly what has come into question today because of serious questions around the credibility and trustworthiness of a church institution that protects clerical abusers and insists on keeping the laity in a position of, as it were, radical dependence.

In 1974 Chenu addresses Rahner's contrast between sign and symbol, admitting that "I have some difficulty in dissociating symbol and sign because, whatever I do, I am Augustinian."[6] A sign is here an arbitrarily assigned association with an exterior nature, in which A points to B. A symbol is, by contrast, a "manifestation," a "symbolized reality itself." Would it be too arrogant to choose symbols and assign new meaning, or a range of meanings? What if, instead, symbols that carry defined significances that vary among world cultures and time periods are mined for their meaning and then used in other contexts—does this amount to a broad and generous openness to the richness and diversity of human symbolic perception, or does it venture too close to cultural misappropriation?

From this perspective, communities or individuals may be told that they cannot invent symbol, in other words, that it must be received. But that opens the question of where a symbol's assigned meaning originates—in a patriarchal worldview that does not represent the wider range of human experience of the divine? Can a symbol negate a community's lived experience by misrepresenting concrete realities or silencing already hesitant voices?

For restless women, symbols are powerful, rooted in nature, but can be improvised, discovered in the community's immediate environment, and brought forth to meet contemporary situations and dilemmas. There was an energetic and enthusiastic embrace of the opportunity to discover new symbols and use them in shared prayer and women's liturgies. One example comes from the UK "Catholic Women's Network" Easter Triduum liturgies at Noddfa Centre in Wales in the early 2000s. As part of the Good Friday liturgy we made a pilgrimage on the grounds that ended in one of the garages, where several women participants, marked with ashes, lay on their backs with their feet in the air in a posture of death. It was the year when foot and mouth disease had ravaged farms in the UK and great numbers of

6. Chenu 1974, par. 27.

sheep and cattle were slaughtered to prevent the spread of the disease. Physically symbolizing the slaughter of the innocent sheep concretized the shock and tragedy of Good Friday.

Another striking example of a symbolic action that produced a profound effect in its use in liturgy took place at an international gathering of women at De Tiltenberg, a Grail retreat house in the Netherlands. When the congregation entered the gathering space, all of the four-legged stools used for seating had been turned upside down. Their spiky legs poked up threateningly in the air, as if a stumble could bring them crashing down and cause injury. But it didn't. Instead, everyone was invited to take hold of the stools and turn them right side up—to turn them into inviting seating to create a safe space where people could sit and relax. An anti-symbol, or negative symbol, was turned easily into a safe, positive, affirming symbol.

Janet Martin Soskice speaks of "turning the symbols."[7] She lists symbolic features sought by feminist Christians in their liturgical celebrations: "affirmation of bodily existence, inter-connectedness, concern for the created order, [and] the holiness of the everyday."[8] Further, she points out that symbols can be just as arbitrary as signs. "They vary from culture to culture, they shift over time, they turn and they can be turned. Symbols, like languages themselves, are social products and not natural kinds. . . . And even shared symbols are not necessarily univocal."[9] What this implies is that any symbol used in religious observance can carry multiple significances, and can be perceived as positive or negative, helpful or a stumbling block, in different cultures and communities. Take, for example, the symbolic gesture by which, according to the Roman Missal, the priest receives the Body and Blood of Christ at the altar before coming forward to distribute Communion to members of the congregation. In 1991, at a conference on the inculturation of the liturgy held at the Pontifical Institute of San Anselmo, I heard the eminent liturgist Anscar Chupungco explain that this is offensive to Filipino Christians—it violates the rules of gracious and appropriate hospitality. The host does not eat first, in front of the guests.

7. Janet Martin Soskice, "Turning the Symbols," in Daphne Hampson, ed. *Swallowing a Fishbone? Feminist Theologians Debate Christianity* (London: SPCK, 1996): 17–32.

8. Soskice, "Turning the Symbols," 22.

9. Soskice, 27.

Interestingly, today many of the house church communities and reform movement-linked worshiping communities, as well as numerous Protestant congregations, do the same thing: Communion is offered to the people first, and the presider communes last of all.

Feminist theologians have differed in their assessment of the potential for traditional Christian symbols, whether visual or aural, to be transformed into life-giving channels of a living faith in a just and trustworthy God. Some would say that the patriarchal embedding of Christianity makes this an unwieldy task, not to say impossible. Others, though, successfully create new powerful sources of spiritual nourishment and connectedness precisely by experimenting with old symbols, as the women on retreat at Noddfa Centre did, or by using common objects to enact compelling new insights and ways of healing and giving hope. All of this testifies to the power of symbol that Chenu discerned, using the mental categories and constructs of his own time and his own theological training. Chenu was on to something after all.

Tradition

The key questions posed by feminist liturgy scholar Marjorie Procter-Smith thirty years ago still ring true anytime a theologian or liturgist speaks in too facile a manner of tradition as an absolute. Procter-Smith proposed that women and other marginalized Christians raise the question, "Whose tradition is it?"[10] Who had a voice in actively shaping the tradition? Did women, for example, have any voice in forming the tradition? Or were women only expected to teach it to children and not raise too many incisive questions?

In fact women have been allowed to study Roman Catholic theology only for roughly the past seventy-five years. In the 1950s when Christiane Brusselmans was encouraged by her father, a law professor in Leuven, to study theology, a few theology professors would not allow a woman in class. She was allowed to sit the examinations for the courses she took, but was not informed of her grades. At a certain point she discovered that her grades "were not so bad," and she transferred to the

10. Procter-Smith, *In Her Own Rite*, 1–24. See also Susan A. Ross, *Extravagant Affections: A Feminist Sacramental Theology* (New York: Continuum, 1998). Chenu refers to "divine tradition" among other places, in 1947, par. 2, and 1967, par. 8.

Institut Catholique in Paris and earned a *maîtrise*. She later completed a PhD at The Catholic University in Washington, DC.

This means that for some 1900 years of evolution in the theology of the Western church, no women were educated to participate in the development of the tradition. No women took an informed role in theological disputations. No women composed the texts that were taken up into official liturgical books. No women theologians articulated the meaning of the sacraments from their own life realities. Interestingly, in the twentieth century one provocative insight raised concerning the sacraments was the position that each of the sacraments represented an activity or responsibility conventionally assigned to women, but in the sacraments was "cleaned up" and made holy by the hands and words of male clerics. Baptism in water and the Spirit was a clerical version of giving birth in water, blood, and pain. Eucharist represented a meal prepared by women, often requiring considerable labor. Reconciliation is what a woman might effect in a quarreling family or with unruly children; anointing of the sick meant bedside care for invalids and the seriously ill, and so forth.

A second key question posed by Procter-Smith is even more challenging: "Is it true for us?" In the first half of the twentieth century, "Catholic truth" was a byword, and Chenu makes brief reference to the "truth" of the faith as a given. What if it is not a universal truth? What if the lived experiences, understandings, perceptions, and even meaningful symbols vary to the point where what is true in one context or for one defined grouping of persons, does not hold water for others?

Loyola of Chicago professor Susan A. Ross, in *Extraordinary Affections*,[11] raises thought-provoking questions about women and sacramentality that take "Is it true for us?" into deeper ground, particularly on sacramentality and the female body. My own research on a now-defunct blessing rite of the Roman Catholic Church administered only to women,[12] carried out at the same time as Dutch researchers such

11. Ross, *Extravagant Affections*, 74–75.

12. Susan K. Roll, "The Old Rite of the Churching of Women After Childbirth," in Kristin De Troyer, Judith A. Herbert, Judith Ann Johnson, and Anne-Marie Korte, eds., *Wholly Women, Holy Blood: A Feminist Critique of Purity and Impurity* (Harrisburg, PA: Trinity Press, 2003), 117–42.

as Grietje Dresen[13] and Marian Wisse,[14] illustrates by way of example how the old rite of the churching of women after childbirth rests on a primordial revulsion toward women's blood flow after childbirth, and the perceived necessity of a purification rite. The rite's purpose was explained through the centuries in different ways. During the Enlightenment, its purpose was to instruct the woman so that she would raise a pious God-fearing child; in the nineteenth century, the apologetic was that "the woman herself really wants to come to church to give thanks for her survival and that of the child." In the twentieth century, the rite gradually died out from disuse when women, and some priests, simply refused to do it, often defying social pressure in Catholic communities. All through church history the custom of a new mother staying outside the church for weeks after childbirth, then being reintroduced by a rite at the hands of a priest, was coupled with strenuous denial that this had anything to do with ritual purification as legislated for the Hebrew people in the book of Leviticus. Yet women themselves perceived that the church associated childbirth with ritual impurity, sin, and guilt, even when the texts were in Latin. The rite died out when enough of them in different countries said, "No."

For theologians the newer research and thinking around women's bodies and the holy should raise questions about how we actualize our belief in the nature of incarnation, a primary reference point for Chenu. Does the church, even without admitting as much, still operate under the assumption that women's bodies contaminate sacred places, vessels, acts, and words? Is this part of the reason that recent popes have declared the admission of women to all ministries to be a "closed door"? Do we still believe, without expressing the idea openly, that women's bodies somehow pollute what is holy?

When feminists such as Rosemary Radford Ruether reclaimed the pronouncement of the ancient church fathers that "what is not assumed, is not redeemed," they drew the conclusion that Jesus the Christ could not have been made incarnate only in the flesh marked

13. Grietje Dresen, "Better Blood: On Sacrifice and the Churching of New Mothers in the Roman Catholic Tradition," in De Troyer et. al, *Wholly Women, Holy Blood*, n.p.

14. Marian Wisse, "De kerkgang van de moeder na de geboorte van een kind," MA thesis, University of Utrecht, 1984.

by the XY chromosome—that is, male flesh. If so, only biological males would be redeemed by the death and resurrection of Christ, not biological females or anyone else with a variant chromosomal makeup. Soskice raises the question, "If women cannot represent Christ, can Christ represent women? Is Christ to be only the saviour of men? . . . The soteriological weight of the doctrine of the incarnation lies in the assertion that God became 'Man,' to use the older term, not that God became a male."[15] Yet, the Theology of the Body of Pope John Paul II points toward an absolute dichotomy between male and female. But Christ had to have been incarnate in human flesh, not only XY flesh. And what are the implications for women's baptismal call to ministry?

Inculturation of the Liturgy

In 1967 Chenu affirms human persons as the "actors of the liturgy and thereby continuators of the mystery."[16] He makes reference to the text in *Gaudium et Spes* 58 on the process of adopting aspects of various cultures in liturgical celebrations, in effect, the inculturation of the liturgy. The spread of the term "inculturation" affirmed the legitimacy and necessity of interpreting the full range of liturgical practices and symbols in terms of the lived reality of those people.

In the 1970s and 80s the need for a thoroughgoing adaptation of the liturgy and sacramental theology to the realities of women's lives led easily to a comparison with the concept of the inculturation of the liturgy. This tendency went through a sharp turnaround spurred by a paper presented at the 1987 conference of Societas Liturgica in York, England, by the eminent Catholic feminist liturgical scholar Teresa Berger.[17] Berger made a convincing and cogent argument for the multiplicity of women's cultures, and in doing so, recalled the trans-

15. Soskice, "Turning the Symbols," 26.

16. Chenu 1967, par. 7.

17. Teresa Berger, "The Women's Movement as a Liturgical Movement: A Form of Inculturation?," *Studia Liturgica* 20, no. 1 (March 1990), https://journals.sagepub.com/doi/10.1177/003932079002000106 (accessed February 12, 2024). See also Teresa Berger, *Women's Ways of Worship: Gender Analysis and Liturgical History* (Collegeville, MN: Liturgical Press, 1999).

formation made in the late 1970s when Black women, unable to find the realities of their lives and their peoples' histories in the developing feminist Christian movement, coined the term "womanist" to name their distinctive modalities of culture and their particular context for reform. Spanish-speaking feminists would do much the same using the term "mujerista."

In effect this resulted in a needed and healthy repudiation of the idea of one universal normative culture, be it a patriarchal governing culture, or a single "culture" of women. A multiplicity of cultures, and the dynamic nature of cultures that were themselves continually adapting to changed conditions, reshaped the concept of how the liturgy might look and feel different if excluded categories of persons could come front and center as full, active agents of liturgy.

Berger wrote in the same article that the feminist Liturgical Movement is "based on the recognition of the far-ranging invisibility of women in the traditional liturgy (which is no longer a matter of dispute). . . . That the traditional invisibility of women in the liturgy is a matter not of the accidents of historical development, but of a deeply-embedded androcentrism is something which—to cite just one example—the consequences of the menstrual taboo for the status of women in worship make clear—consequences such as the postponement of baptism for women during menstruation, prohibition of access to the altar area, and warnings against communion during menstruation." These practices were consistent with the exclusion of new mothers from the church building until they had undergone the old rite of churching, as explained above.

History

Finally, a note on *ressourcement.* Returning to the ancient original sources as a touchstone in healthy and authentic reform in the present did not happen for the first time in the twentieth century: Martin Luther argued for the necessity of a return to Scripture as a guarantor of authentic theology and worship in the present, to the point of claiming that *sola scriptura* was the only trustworthy criterion. And rediscovering how our early ancestors in faith came together to hear the word and break the bread, not to mention how to baptize new believers and deal with public sinners, proved foundational for the healthy and much-needed liturgical reforms begun at Vatican II.

Yet history, at whatever stage and with whatever subject matter, represents an interpretation of data on past events with their causes and outcomes. Who does the interpreting, and in whose voice? Which voices are not being heard? Which documents disappeared or were destroyed, or simply not valued enough to be preserved? If, as Chenu wrote, "The sacrament is the intermediary between mystery and history,"[18] whose history is meant? Still, there is no guarantee that women historians will reinterpret from the underside, as it were, if they follow the dominant paradigms, consciously or unconsciously. We tend to see what we have been conditioned to see, unless and until some new insight presses its point and creates a fundamental rethinking of what we took for granted. The ideology of patriarchal entitlement and the "maleness" of God the Father is one example.

In the end, we may be left with Chenu's insightful and energizing rethinking of the theological framework of liturgy and sacraments in his own cultural context and his own times, and seeing what results by laying them up against a different time, a global range of contexts, and a passion for a church that makes justice for the poor and the marginalized. This effort may not be entirely fair to Chenu. But perhaps it provides some markers of where we are going, and how liturgy and sacramental spirituality can be brought into dialogue with those who seek and search for well-founded, well-embodied, and rich spiritual meaning today.

18. Chenu 1967, par. 38.

Pastoral Liturgical Perspectives

Samuel Goyvaerts

Clearly, Marie-Dominique Chenu is not a pastoral theologian or pastoral liturgist. Nevertheless, he is writing during a time when the Liturgical Movement has led to the emergence of pastoral liturgy as a distinct discipline and a specialized approach to studying liturgy and the sacraments, particularly in Paris. Here, one of Chenu's fellow Dominican friars, Aimon-Marie Roguet (1906–1991), co-founded and directed the Centre de Pastorale Liturgique in 1943.[1] So although neither a pastoral theologian nor a liturgist, in his reflections on liturgy and anthropology one can find interesting ideas when reading from a contemporary pastoral liturgical perspective. While all liturgical studies have the liturgy as it subject, pastoral liturgy specifically emphasizes the theological and practical dimensions of the liturgical rites in a pastoral context. It emphasizes the relationship between theological reflection and pastoral praxis in the context of the liturgy, but also explores the relation of the liturgy with Christian life as a whole.[2]

1. See Benoît-Marie Solaberrieta, "Les experts du Centre de Pastorale Liturgique," in *Liturgie et société*, ed. Bruno Dumons, Vincent Petit, and Christian Sorrel (Rennes: Presses universitaires de Rennes, 2016), https://doi.org/10.4000/books.pur.46833.

2. See Samuel Goyvaerts, "Moving between Liturgical Theology and Liturgical Pastoral: On Theology, Liturgy, and Christian Life," *Questions Liturgiques* 100, nos. 1–2 (2020): 294–312; Samuel Goyvaerts, "Liturgy and Pastoral Ministry," in J. Geldhof, ed., *Cambridge Companion to Christian Liturgy* (Cambridge University Press, forthcoming).

For this contribution, I will start by briefly discussing these passages in which Chenu explicitly mentions a pastoral-liturgical dimension. Subsequently, I have selected three specific themes coming up in his writings which touch pastoral liturgical studies. First, I will discuss the anthropological turn Chenu makes and his stress on the bodily dimension of the liturgy. From this follows secondly, his symbol theory, in which he stresses the "human realism" of the liturgy, closely connected to a plea for inculturated liturgy. Third and last, I will show how the connection Chenu makes between liturgy and imagination is also of particular interest for pastoral liturgical studies. Other pastoral liturgical themes present in his writings on which I will not elaborate are the dynamics between community and individual when it comes down to the liturgy and the importance of formation and (mystagogical) catechesis. First however, a brief general overview after careful study of the articles presented in this volume.

Chenu on Pastoral Liturgy

In the 1947 article and starting from its anthropological dimension, Chenu considers the liturgy to be fundamentally pastoral: "Pastoral therefore by definition, it is nourished by tradition, both divine tradition and valuable human traditions, without giving in to archeologism."[3] Already here in this brief quotation, we are confronted with one of the main points in his thinking: the interrelatedness between divine and human, in this case its traditions. Although being pastoral in its core, the liturgy consists of and reveals the content of Christian tradition, according to Chenu. In the same article, when reflecting on the communal dimension of the liturgy and its relation to sociology, Chenu concludes that a great task is waiting here for pastoral liturgy, since the rebirth of the Christian community and the rebirth of the liturgy go hand in hand.[4] Both these ideas, the relation between practical forms and theological content on the one hand, and the relation between liturgy and *koinonia* or church community on the other hand, align perfectly well with the fundamental convic-

3. Chenu 1947, par. 2.
4. Chenu 1947, par. 24.

tions and ambitions of the Liturgical Movement. Chenu also refers to the Centre de Pastorale Liturgique conference which he apparently attended. These conferences were important events for spreading the ideas of the Liturgical Movement.[5]

In the 1952 article, Chenu situates pastoral ministry and liturgy in the economy of salvation, which is the topic of the article. It is time, according to Chenu, to retrieve "the historical and temporal element . . . in the structure of the mystery and the Christian rite" which is urgent and needs a rebalancing both in view of "an orthodoxy of truth and for an effective pastoral practice."[6] This is an intriguing statement, in particular when one makes the connection between truth and liturgy, understood as "doxa," which means "praise." As such, Chenu appears to align with the adage "*lex orandi, lex credendi*": the manner of prayer shapes one's faith. Chenu demonstrates how the experience of the Christian faith, liturgical practices, and pastoral engagement are inherently connected to theology and should be taken seriously—not merely as practical applications of dogma and doctrine, but as genuine sources of theology and even salvific revelation.

For Chenu, it should also be pastoral consciousness which urges us to pay attention to what he calls "the temporal economy of the mystery."[7] The relation between supernatural grace and the human dimension of the liturgy and the sacraments is a reoccurring theme in all the articles studied, and also the background of his reflections on symbol and mystery, to which I will return. The double dimension of the liturgical symbol, both divine and human, is crucial for liturgical practice.[8] In the conclusion of the 1952 article Chenu formulates it as follows, again explicitly referring to the pastoral liturgical dimension: "The Christian celebration is therefore the exact emanation of the economy of salvation." He relates this emanation of salvation explicitly to the sacramental symbolism of the liturgy. For him, it

5. Chenu 1947, par. 23.

6. Chenu 1952, par. 1–2.

7. Chenu 1952, par. 25–27.

8. Chenu 1952, par. 31: "It will therefore be necessary to maintain, both in the understanding of the symbol and in its liturgical practice, the right balance of this double symbolic framework, distinct and so linked at the same time."

becomes uniquely clear in the liturgy how sensuality and materiality—earthliness—can signify and bear divine life. Chenu closes this article with this joining of divine and earthly things, writing: "The liturgy finds its light there, and pastoral ministry the rule of its efficacy."[9] These ideas of the 1952 article on the double nature of the symbol and how it enables participation in the divine mystery, which has practical liturgical consequences and constitutes pastoral action, are repeated and elaborated on also in the 1967 and 1974 articles.

These few paragraphs are the explicit statements of Chenu on the field of practical or pastoral liturgy, but of course many of the ideas he discusses can be appropriated from a pastoral liturgical perspective and challenge contemporary pastoral liturgical reflection.

The Anthropological Turn and the Bodily Dimension of the Liturgy

Stressing the historical, human dimension of Christianity and its worship—as I have just shown—also leads Chenu to warn about the dangers of dehumanizing or spiritualizing the liturgy, which has irrevocably happened in the history of the Christian liturgy. In his time, Chenu calls for the necessary "anthropological turn" in liturgy and symbol theory underpinning sacramental theology. According to Chenu, Vatican II has not yet developed a good anthropology, but science and society have already made this turn and it is time for theology and the church to do the same.[10] Not just because the church has to follow modern society, but because this anthropological dimension is inherent to the Christian mystery itself. Chenu calls this the "the original realism" of the mystery, showing that the "human being is not a spirit lodged in a body, it is a being where the body is consubstantially united with the spirit."[11] Also in other passages of the articles presented in this volume, he reacts against

9. Chenu 1952, par. 33.

10. Chenu 1967, par. 2; also compare Crispino Valenziano, "Liturgy and Anthropology: The Meaning of the Question and the Method for Answering It," in Anscar J. Chupungco, ed., *Handbook for Liturgical Studies, Volume II: Fundamental Liturgy* (Collegeville, MN: Liturgical Press, 1998), 189–224, esp. 192.

11. Chenu 1967, par. 7.

spiritualizing tendencies in Christianity and against neglecting or even depreciating the human and bodily dimension of Christian religion in general and the liturgy in particular. This is very much aligned with what Charles Taylor in his famous book, *The Secular Age,* calls excarnation.[12] For Taylor as well as for Chenu it is the incarnation that marks the uniqueness of Christian religion and its particular form or worship, which Chenu distinguishes from "religion which emanates from the nature of humanity."[13] A God who enters history installs a completely different relation between human and divine, aptly coined by Chenu as "deification is done by and in the humanization of God."[14]

Throughout this article, and long before theologians like Chauvet, Chenu stresses the importance of the body in worship: "Worship includes in its very substance the reality, burdensome and exciting, of the life of the body, with all its components. This corporeality, in all its forms and according to its own laws, is really the cause, and not only the condition, of the human and sacred intensity of the liturgical act."[15] This great importance of the body has been constantly emphasized by various theologians over the past fifty or sixty years. At the same time, and here I come to my more pastoral liturgical reflections, in the liturgical reform after Vatican II, the emphasis was nevertheless mainly on the texts, both the design of new texts and especially the translation of the Latin typical editions, which to this day seems to be the main task of many liturgical commissions. To give this physical dimension—at least to my knowledge of the celebrating communities in the northern hemisphere—sufficient attention in education, liturgy training programs, and, unfortunately, also in the actual celebration of the liturgy, seems to be very difficult. Although the postconciliar liturgy and their

12. See Charles Taylor, *A Secular Age* (Cambridge, MA: Harvard University Press, 2007), 613–15. Also see Samuel Goyvaerts, "De excarnatie voorbij: Over de blijvende relevantie van de lichamelijke dimensie van de liturgie," in *Over de hardnekkige aanwezigheid van het christendom,* ed. Samuel Goyvaerts, Kess de Groot, and Jos Pieper, Utrechtste Studies, vol. XXIII (Parthenon: Almere, 2020), 66–82.

13. Chenu 1967, par. 14.

14. Chenu 1967, par. 15. The same movement is more recently described by David Fagerberg, among others, see David W. Fagerberg, *Consecrating the World: On Mundane Liturgical Theology* (Kettering, OH: Angelico Press, 2016).

15. Chenu 1967, par. 18

rubrics do provide for this, there remains an undervaluation or at least a lack of attention to the bodily dimension of worship. To name just one example, well-known to liturgists in my part of the world: communities in which the congregation visits in procession the four foreseen places of the ritual of baptism, namely the entrance to the church, ambo, baptismal font, and altar, and performs the corresponding liturgical acts at these "physical places" in the church building, are very few or nonexistent. Especially in a time and society in which non-textual elements claim their place, where attention and care for the body, and body-mind experiences seem to reign supreme, liturgy can and should nurture and promote what Chenu calls the burdensome and exciting reality of the life of the body.[16] Chenu's anthropological turn clearly poses an urgent challenge for contemporary pastoral liturgics, but also has consequences for his symbol theory.

Human Realism of the Symbol and Inculturated Liturgy

From the 1952 article onwards, Chenu stresses what he calls the "naturalism" or the "human realism" of the symbol.[17] The "natural" quality of the symbol guarantees that it is a logical and sound representation of the mystery. The example Chenu uses refers to the Eucharist and eating of food: transforming or even removing the rites of presenting and eating the food does not at all mean that we have a better spiritual communion with Christ's sacrifice. Again, Chenu warns against spiritualization and ignoring the human and bodily dimension of liturgy, sacrament, and symbol. Even more, revaluing this dimension is the only way, in his view, to revitalize the liturgy, which was exactly what the pastoral liturgical efforts of the Liturgical Movement intended to do. At the same time, Chenu is not concerned here with some whim of modernity, but with the essence of the Christian mystery itself. This is linked to the incarnation and it belongs to the essence of Christian faith to embody the sacred, what Chenu calls "the logic of the humanization of the mystery."[18]

16. Compare Chenu 1967, par. 18.
17. Chenu 1952, par. 31.
18. Chenu 1967, par. 16.

This "humanization of the mystery" requires important discernment according to Chenu, where there should be no fear of losing something of the sacred in renewing symbols, action, gestures, and words. In other words, this also questions the way we shape our liturgical symbols, action, gestures, and words. To take up the example of the Eucharist again: do these small white wafers indeed represent our daily bread, which is presented, thanked for, broken, and given for all? [19] Do those few drops of baptismal water still evoke the experience of washing, or even stronger, of drowning, dying, and rising again? Has liturgical tradition indeed eliminated some of the naturalism of our symbols, which hampers the liturgical imagination needed to understand and experience liturgy? Although very practical liturgical questions as such, this is not just a question of anthropology or cultural adaptation but a serious, also theological, matter which has to do with the essence of sacramentality itself. When the sacraments are "dehumanized" their nature itself is neglected according to Chenu, and the future of the liturgy depends on the figurative symbolization of the mystery.[20] Chenu is aware that this is an exciting challenge, in which one must not disregard the dialectic between divine mystery and human form.[21] On the one hand, things are separated from their day-to-day "secular" use. In the liturgy they are transfigured into symbols and gestures of the sacred—Chenu uses the word "theophany." On the other hand, they cannot become completely alienated from human or wordly existence; the symbols, action, gestures, and words used for liturgy and sacraments must remain recognizable and their original—what Chenu calls "natural"—meaning must remain perceptible.

In the same vain and logically flowing from his reflections on symbolic representation of the mystery, Chenu also speaks about inculturation, referring not to *Sacrosanctum Concilium* 37–40 in this case but to *Gaudium et Spes* 58. He was of course involved in the redaction

19. Chenu 1967, par. 20. Also compare Thomas O'Loughlin, "Celebrating Synodality: Synodality as a Fundamental Aspect of Christian Liturgy," *New Blackfriars* 104 (2023): 161–78, here 177, https://doi.org/10.1111/nbfr.12807.

20. Chenu 1967, par. 20.

21. Chenu 1967, par. 26.

process of this dogmatic constitution.[22] This remains, until today, a massive challenge for the church on the pastoral liturgical level. I am not only referring here to the Zairean rite or an—until today non-existent—Amazonian rite. An equally important challenge in view of inculturation, in particular for a Western context, is how to inculturate the liturgy in a secular, desacralized cultural context.[23] Which natural "symbols" to manifest the incarnated mystery can be found in a culture which has declared the death of God?

In recent years a more dynamic and broader view on inculturation of the liturgy was developed; see, for example, the Nairobi statement on inculturation of the Lutheran World Federation:

> Christian worship relates dynamically to culture in at least four ways. First, it is transcultural, the same substance for everyone everywhere, beyond culture. Second, it is contextual, varying according to the local situation (both nature and culture). Third, it is counter-cultural, challenging what is contrary to the Gospel in a given culture. Fourth, it is cross-cultural, making possible sharing between different local cultures. In all four dynamics, there are helpful principles which can be identified. [24]

The third and fourth dimensions, counter-cultural and cross-cultural, do not so easily fit in the framework of Chenu's thinking. It shows how time and the perspective on the relation between culture and Christianity since *Gaudium et Spes* has changed. It is clear the question of inculturation is very complex and culture itself is multi-diverse, for example, with a still growing fast food consumerism on the one hand, and strong "woke" convictions in view of what to eat and what most definitely not to consume on the other hand. A culture which is

22. For the quotation from GS see Chenu 1967, par. 7; other references to inculturation: Chenu 1967, par. 19. Also see footnote 2 of the text.

23. On liturgy in a secular context, also see Joris Geldhof, *Liturgy and Secularism: Beyond the Divide* (Collegeville, MN: Liturgical Press, 2018).

24. Lutheran World Federation, "Nairobi Statement on Worship and Culture: Contemporary Challenges and Opportunities," *Studia Liturgica*, 27, no. 1 (1997): 88–93. Also see Joris Geldhof, "Inculturation dans le domaine liturgique: défauts et défis d'un concept contesté," *La Maison-Dieu* 296 (2019): 35–52.

highly individualized, much more than Chenu could have ever imagined in 1967, but at the same time giving access to global connectivity and a relentless search for interconnectedness; a culture in which the traditional family meal is still a crucial place of encounter, but also hosting divorced, gender-diffuse, and blended families. More than ever, I believe, together with Chenu, it is the task of pastoral liturgy, based on cultural and anthropological research, to both experiment and reflect on how an inculturated liturgy receives its shape. In this respect, I would like to refer to the method of pastoral liturgical studies already presented by Mark Searle (1941–1992), who unfortunately died far too early and is therefore probably less well known.[25] In 1983, Searle published an article on the task and mission of liturgical studies, especially pastoral liturgy. Starting from a synchronous approach to liturgy, he sees a threefold task for pastoral liturgical studies: an empirical, a hermeneutical, and a critical one. Summarized, the first task is the empirical, merely describing what happens in liturgy. Searle refers both to sociology—for the empirical method—and to anthropology—for the study of liturgy as a ritual. For the second, hermeneutical task of pastoral liturgy, Searle focuses on the way in which the symbolic words and actions of the liturgy function. This mainly concerns the effectiveness of liturgical symbols to communicate the mystery of God's grace on the one hand and about the capacity of contemporary people to be open to this kind of communication on the other, very much like what Chenu develops more theoretically. According to Searle, this kind of study can form a basis for improving the ritual itself and especially its execution, but also for developing evangelization and catechesis. The third task, the critical one, is to examine the results of the two preceding ones, the empirical and the hermeneutical, in the light of tradition and theology. According to Searle, recognizing the normativity of the theological tradition is therefore not only what distinguishes pastoral liturgy from its auxiliary disciplines, such as sociology, but is also conditional in view of the sacramental character of the economy of salvation. It is this last task that makes pastoral liturgy

25. Mark Searle, "New Tasks, New Methods: The Emergence of Pastoral Liturgical Studies," *Worship* 57, no. 4 (1983): 291–308. On pastoral liturgy and Searle, also see Goyvaerts, "Moving between Liturgical Theology," 301–3.

a true theological discipline. Thus described, pastoral liturgy requires a high degree of interdisciplinary work, of which Searle is well-aware.

Both Searle and Chenu advocate combining meaningful and important symbols and values of contemporary people with the normative and sacred dimension of the liturgical tradition. This is easier said than done of course, I realize. Among other things, this will require a new attention to religious and liturgical imagination, a third point on which Chenu challenges pastoral liturgical studies.

Liturgical Imagination

The liturgy obviously belongs to the order of signification, which Chenu discerns from explanation.[26] The liturgical act cannot be reduced to an explanation, nor to knowledge or straightforward development; it does not depend on analyzing or deduction, but on an "initiation through participation" according to Chenu. Both initiation and participation are other important fields of pastoral liturgical studies, which I cannot explore in the framework of this contribution. Instead, I focus on liturgical imagination. Meanings, including liturgical meanings, work with images that cannot be rationalized and have to do with human sensory faculties. Evidently, reason is important and essential for human beings, but according to Chenu reason always obtains its knowledge and ideas from an "intelligence immersed in the sensible."[27]

In this realm of images and imagination, the symbol is, according to Chenu, the crucial representation of the sacred and of the Christian mystery celebrated in the liturgy. In relation to the symbol and symbolic thinking, the imagination plays a decisive role in the mental act which is needed to go from signifier to signified. Thanks to the imagination, the symbol is able to effect this necessary leap or transfer: "the symbol, spoken or acted, proceeds from a metaphor, that is to say from a transfer by which the spirit, imagination and intelligence,

26. Chenu 1967, par. 31. Also see Samuel Goyvaerts, "Symbols and Senses: Imagination and the Modern Incapability of the Liturgical Act," in D. Minch and P. I. Okpaleke, eds., *Imagination and Dialogue,* Explorations at the Crossroads of Theology and Aesthetics series (London: T&T Clark, forthcoming).

27. Chenu 1967, par. 31.

passes, by a kind of provocation, from one reality to another, thanks to their analogy."[28] Briefly summarized, Chenu states that human being is determined by being in the world, which becomes very clear in the human activity of signifying. Signifying happens through an interplay between the physical or sensory and the rational, with the imagination acting as a kind of bridge, thus identified as one of the essential faculties of human being. Liturgy lies in the realm of signifying, in which the power of the imagination is necessary in order to gain meaningful access to the sensual-symbolic actions; it is almost literally "making sense." This is a matter of a real and active "participating in" and not merely by way of grasping or understanding, which is a very important distinction.

Here again, we can draw parallels to the ideas of the aforementioned American pastoral liturgical scholar Mark Searle. Departing from the normativity of the theological tradition, Searle claimed that pastoral liturgy must be critical of itself, critical of contemporary culture, as well as looking critically at various forms of religious imagination. After all, "[I]t is through the imagination, rather than through professed beliefs and conscious attitudes, that religious understanding and behavior are filtered."[29] I think this is a crucial statement for all those professionally involved in liturgy, or for this matter, theology. The imagination is the most important human capacity when it comes to faith and liturgical celebration, which Chenu also explained. It is not the exact following of rubrics, the fathoming of liturgical history, the rational understanding of the belief system, or unlimited liturgical creativity that shapes faith and liturgical experience, but the imagination. In doing so, it is important to realize that liturgy and Scripture, Searle claims, not only constitute the religious imagination, but are themselves filtered and understood through the religious imagination. It is an important task of pastoral liturgy "to compare the imaginative world projected by the liturgy with the imaginative world out of which North Americans operate."[30] This comparison and theological reflection can help identify common misunderstandings, on the one

28. Chenu 1967, par. 32.
29. Searle, "New Tasks, New Methods," 303.
30. Searle, "New Tasks, New Methods," 304.

hand, and benefit inculturation, on the other. More importantly, it is crucial to be aware that there is a liturgical imagination *an sich* presented in and through the liturgy *qua* liturgy on the one hand and the liturgical imagination of those who celebrate the liturgy on the other. How liturgical symbols, words, and gestures interact with the religious imagination of contemporary human beings is a vital question for the future of pastoral liturgical studies.[31]

Conclusion

In the beginning of the article on liturgical anthropology Chenu claims: "Today's humanity poses new questions to the Church, to the Church's liturgy—as well as to catechesis and theology."[32] Some of these questions are taken up in the process of the synodal movement, and recent ecclesial documents like *Fiducia supplicans*,[33] but both of these examples also show how much theological groundwork still has to be done in view of these questions. According to Pope Francis, a paradigm shift in theology is needed for theology to become "a fundamentally contextual theology, capable of reading and interpreting the Gospel in the conditions in which men and women daily live."[34] For pastors and theologians alike, it remains a question and a challenge to reflect on the relation between the liturgical and theological tradition, and the questions of humanity and the world. The entire ecological question for example is a subject that Chenu—and his time—understandably do not really consider. The human being as a human being in one's environment, the relationship with the world and one's dealings with it, how this translates in and connects to liturgy is also a pastoral

31. Also see Thomas H. Schattauer, "Training Liturgical Imagination," *Living Lutheran: Short paper at NAAL Conference 2023*, https://www.livinglutheran.org/2019/12/training-liturgical-imagination/ (accessed July 16, 2024).

32. Chenu 1967, par. 9.

33. Dicastery for the Doctrine of the Faith, *Declaration Fiducia Supplicans*, On the Pastoral Meaning of Blessings, December 18, 2023, https://www.vatican.va/roman_curia/congregations/cfaith/documents/rc_ddf_doc_20231218_fiducia-supplicans_en.html.

34. Pope Francis, *Motu proprio Ad theologiam promovendam*, November 1, 2023, https://www.vatican.va/content/francesco/it/motu_proprio/documents/20231101-motu-proprio-ad-theologiam-promovendam.html.

liturgical challenge.[35] Nevertheless, a fundamental theological basis on how to deal with these new questions can already be found in the work of Chenu, stressing the dimensions of the body, symbol, and the imagination for pastoral liturgy and theology.

35. E.g., Kevin W. Irwin, *Ecology, Liturgy, and the Sacraments* (Mahwah, NJ: Paulist Press, 2023).

Afterword

The Myriad Chenu: Rereading the World as Sacrament

Karim Schelkens

Whoever studies the *ressourcement* that has shaped twentieth-century Catholic theology has, without any doubt, come across the name of Marie-Dominique Chenu.[1] Yet, in contrast to many of his contemporaries, his image remains slippery, difficult to grasp. This is already tangible from the difference between two recent biographies devoted to his life and work.[2]

While Étienne Fouilloux portrayed Chenu as a champion of historical thought in the Catholic theological landscape, Michael Quisinsky emphasized the importance of his anthropology, Christology and pneumatology, highlighting the theologian Chenu. And there's more. Next to the historian and the theologian, there's Chenu as the proponent of *nouvelle théologie*; there's the "informal" Vatican II expert who played a role behind the scenes in the leadup to the Pastoral Constitution *Gaudium et Spes,* itself a historical novelty in the conciliar history; there's

1. G. Flynn and P. D. Murray, eds., *Ressourcement: A Movement for Renewal in Twentieth-Century Catholic Theology* (Oxford: Oxford University Press, 2012).

2. It is striking that the study by the historian Étienne Fouilloux, *Marie-Dominique Chenu 1895–1990* (Paris: Éditions Salvator, 2022), strongly identifies Chenu as a champion of "historical" theology, while Michael Quisinsky's *Marie-Dominique Chenu: Weg – Werk – Wirkung* (Freiburg im Breisgau: Verlag Herder, 2021) lays the emphasis on the integral view.

the ecumenically engaged Dominican friar who sided with Christophe Dumont in the outreach to the Orthodox world; there's the rector and innovator of *Le Saulchoir* who saw his writings relegated to the Index;[3] the supporter of the Worker Priest movement; or the diligent re-reader and interpreter of Thomas Aquinas. And one need only consider his influence on figures like the liturgist Odo Casel to come across Chenu the liturgist.[4]

This superficial juxtaposition of images is, of course, a bit misleading. In fact, scholarship on the Second Vatican Council and the half century preceding it increasingly indicates the crossover between the variety of *ressourcement* movements that have shaped the era. The ties of a figure like Chenu with virtually all of these movements are, to that extent, revealing, as they put him at the heart of theological reflection of the previous century. This volume offers a worthy testimony to that, not just by studying his legacy, but also by letting his own work resound. Studying the articles by Chenu published here, the reader is immediately immersed in the richness and depth of his work. The angle taken by the editors, focusing on liturgy and sacraments, is one that has often been neglected—unrightfully so, as it weaves itself as a red thread in Chenu's approach to the various fields in which he was engaged: the experience of the divine within the concrete, historical, and lived experience of human beings.

Reconsidering this as the heart of Chenu's legacy helps, at least, to avoid the pitfall of unilateralism. As a proponent of *nouvelle théologie*, Chenu has often been claimed by church historians as having reintroduced historical thought in theology. Yet, however many historical studies he wrote, the angle was never that of dry historicity. What was at stake was not so much the past, but rather the lingering presence of mystery in past, present, and future experiences of faith. In that regard, the historian Chenu was always a sacramental theologian, his thought was always immersed in what Boersma called "the litur-

3. Étienne Fouilloux, "Autour d'une mise à l'Index," in *Marie-Dominique Chenu, Moyen-Âge et modernité* (Paris: Cerf, 1997), 25–56.

4. Michael Quisinsky, "Échos Allemands à *Une École de Théologie: Le Saulchoir* (1939–1941): Les Réactions de F. Stegmüller, O. Casel et A. Deissler," *Revue des sciences philosophiques et théologiques* 94, no. 1 (2010): 121–32.

gical setting of theology."[5] This is interesting in the light of twentieth-century church history, and it starts long before Chenu's own time.

Étienne Fouilloux's typology of the early twentieth-century modernist crisis as the intellectual matrix for twentieth-century theology is never remote when studying Chenu and the Dominicans of his generation.[6] Those who had witnessed the era of Pius X had been confronted with the simultaneous rise of liturgical reforms and the distrust of biblical scholarship. For a long time, liturgy was enclosed in the "canon law" part of the theological curriculum, and in the field of biblical studies the element of historical contingency was regarded as dangerous from the side of the Catholic hierarchy and tied to the analogy of faith. The focus of church rhetoric was on textuality, and the response given by avant-garde Dominicans like Ambroise Gardeil, and later Chenu, was deeply inspired by the study in historical method written by Lagrange already around the turn of the century.[7]

Lagrange's *methode historique* already sought to integrate the Thomist view of humanity's inherent orientation toward God with a vivid sense of historicity.[8] One might say that what Lagrange did for biblical *ressourcement*, Chenu did for Thomistic *ressourcement*, when exploring how twelfth- and thirteenth-century thinkers perceived the human person in relation to divine grace and the broader cosmos. In the work of both Dominicans, the experience of encounter underlying the textual field was key, and their move "beyond text" was crucial for all of the aforementioned fields of renewal, be they ecumenical, biblical, liturgical, dogmatic, or pastoral. This puts Chenu in a particular position in an

5. Hans Boersma, *Nouvelle Théologie and Sacramental Ontology: A Return to Mystery* (Oxford: Oxford University Press, 2009), 139.

6. Étienne Fouilloux, *Une Église en quête de liberté: La pensée catholique française entre modernisme et Vatican II (1914–1962)* (Paris: Desclée de Brouwer, 1998), 17.

7. Jon Kirwan, *An Avant-garde Theological Generation: The Nouvelle Théologie and the French Crisis of Modernity* (Oxford: Oxford University Press, 2018). On the connection with Gardeil, founder of Le Saulchoir, see Jean Jolivet, "M.D. Chenu. Médiéviste et théologien," *Revue des sciences philosophiques et théologiques* 81 (1997): 381–94. Chenu's rhetoric strongly relied upon Gardeil's *Le donné révélé et la théologie* (Paris: Cerf, 1910), which in turn was indebted to the work of Lagrange.

8. Marie-Joseph Lagrange, *La méthode historique surtout à propos de l'Ancien Testament* (Paris: Lecoffre, 1903).

era shaped not only by Catholic *ressourcement*, but also by dialectical theology in the reformed world. While the Barthian voices of his time underlined the gap between human experience and the revealed word in the biblical canon, opposing mystery to human experience, Chenu's Thomist anthropology offered a contrasting voice. Its awareness of sacraments as vital expressions of the church's engagement with the world, deeply embedded in the historical and cultural contexts of the faithful, allowed for an open stance to the modern world.

The present volume highlights precisely the interwovenness of all the above perspectives and the need for rediscovering holistic perspectives of humanity, world, and cosmos through careful discernment of the signs of the times, also in the twenty-first century.[9] This task cannot be properly carried out without diligent scrutiny of the "embodied" nature of our relatedness to the divine. The reflections offered in the contributions to this volume do precisely that, symbolically bridging the gap between world and worship.

9. Ignace Ndongala Maduku, "Penser le discernement avec M.D. Chenu, J.-M.R. Tillard et C. Theobald: Notes sur une recherche en cours," *Théologiques* 22, no. 2 (2014): 167–78.